THE
SEARCH
FOR
HAPPINESS

OTHER BOOKS
BY FATHER LUKEFAHR

"We Believe..."
A Survey of the Catholic Faith

Christ's Mother and Ours
A Catholic Guide to Mary

The Catechism Handbook

The Privilege of Being Catholic

A Catholic Guide to the Bible

THE
SEARCH
FOR
HAPPINESS

FOUR LEVELS OF EMOTIONAL
AND SPIRITUAL GROWTH

OSCAR LUKEFAHR

Liguori/Triumph
LIGUORI, MISSOURI

Imprimi Potest:
Richard Thibodeau, C.Ss.R.
Provincial, Denver Province
The Redemptorists

Published by Liguori/Triumph
An imprint of Liguori Publications
Liguori, Missouri
www.liguori.org
www.catholicbooksonline.com

Library of Congress Cataloging-in-Publication Data

Lukefahr, Oscar.
    The search for happiness : four levels of emotional and spiritual growth / Oscar Lukefahr.
        p. cm.
    Includes bibliographical references.
    ISBN 0-7648-0932-6 (pbk.)
    1. Happiness—Religious aspects—Catholic Church. 2. Christian life— Catholic authors. I. Title.

BV4647 .J68 L85 2003
248.4'82—dc21   2002075979

Printed in the Unitd States of America
06 05 04 03 02   5 4 3 2 1
First edition

To Mike and Mary Wulfers
This was your idea!

CONTENTS

PREFACE

❧

Everyone wants to be happy. No one wants to be sad. But what is happiness? Is it the result of circumstances? Do pleasure, possessions, popularity, and power guarantee happiness? Do we have any control over whether or not we will be happy?

Several years ago I listened to a recorded talk given to members of the Christian Medical and Dental Associations by Dr. John Patrick, M.D., an internationally known physician and speaker. The talk explained happiness by placing it on four levels, and was based on ideas developed by Father Robert Spitzer, S.J., president of Gonzaga University. Reflecting on the talk helped me understand happiness better by seeing how it exists at each of the four levels. I began to talk about these levels at parish missions, teachers' conferences, diocesan gatherings, and youth retreats. Many people suggested that I should develop the talks into a book, and *The Search For Happiness* is that book.

I am indebted to Dr. Patrick and to Father Spitzer for explaining the four levels of happiness in a clear and compelling manner. In his fine book, *Healing the Culture* (Ignatius Press, San Francisco, 2000), Father Spitzer states that the concept of various levels of happiness goes back to ancient philosophers, both pagan and Christian. It is a notion that is time-tested, and it can help us understand and achieve happiness in our own time.

Readers might ask for my qualifications to write a book on happiness. I'm certainly not "happy-go-lucky." But I am happy, more so after several years of studying the four levels of happiness and striving to implement what they teach. As a Catholic priest, I firmly believe that complete happiness can be found only in God. I see the four levels as a God-given stairway designed to lead us to God. I believe that Jesus Christ is our Model for living the four levels and the one who leads us up that stairway. I've never regretted following Jesus, and I've never heard people say they were unhappy that they had followed Jesus. The four levels as lived by Jesus are part of the Good News that I as a priest want to share. Hence this book.

It should be noted that God has been getting a lot of good press lately from astronomers, physicists, microbiologists, and other scientists. This should add to our excitement and anticipation as we move toward God and God's gift of happiness. More on this later. For now, my prayer is that this book may provide a pattern for understanding happiness and a pathway to the happiness only God can give.

FATHER OSCAR LUKEFAHR, C.M.

ACKNOWLEDGMENTS

S incere thanks to all who helped in the writing of *The Search for Happiness*...to Mike and Mary Wulfers, who brought Dr. Patrick's talk on the four levels of happiness to my attention and encouraged me to write this book; to John Cleary, whose editing, enthusiasm, advice, and suggestions were invaluable; to Cecelia Portlock for her expertise and technical advice in the editing process; to Judy Bauer and Sister Mary Margaret Doorley, who provided direction and support; to Janet Penning, who designed the interior; to Pam Hummelsheim for her talent to create the beautiful cover; to Paul and Carol Berens, Mike and Mary Etta Dunaway, Frank and Gail Jones, and Den and Kathy Vollink, who discussed each chapter at our monthly study group meetings; to Kathy Whittenberger, who proofed the manuscript and made many helpful suggestions; to the Catholic Home Study Service staff, Cheryl Callier, Penny Elder, and Sherrie Hotop, for proofreading, comments, and cheerful assistance.

THE
SEARCH
FOR
HAPPINESS

INTRODUCTION
The Search for Happiness

❧

At a parish mission in Jordan, Montana, a woman told me that her eight-year-old grandson was asked the old catechism question, "Why did God make you?" He replied, "I think God made me to take out the garbage."

Many of us over age fifty remember the real answer: "God made me to know, love, and serve him in this world, and to be happy forever." God made us to be happy. We want to be happy. Happiness should be as natural to us as breathing.

Happiness has been defined as a state of serenity, well-being, and contentment. Albert Schweitzer once said that happiness is nothing more than good health and a bad memory. But no matter how we define happiness, it remains elusive. Many people who seem to have plenty of ingredients for happiness—pleasure, possessions, popularity, and power—are terribly unhappy. Marilyn Monroe and Elvis Presley were among the best-known entertainers of the twentieth century. Both had wealth, fame, status, and access to every kind of pleasure. Yet both were unhappy, and both experienced pathetic, lonely deaths.

If fame, fortune, fun, and influence won't bring happiness, what will? Perhaps the right set of circumstances? Some people think they will be happy if only they have more leisure, or a new job, or a different location, or the right friends. In their view, happiness results from circumstances. A princess will be happy.

A pauper won't. But in the second half of the twentieth century the world met a princess who had everything, and a little nun who owned only two sets of clothing. Princess Diana's life was clouded with unhappiness. Mother Teresa radiated joy.

Circumstances do not guarantee contentment. Happiness is largely up to us. We choose to be happy or sad. We may not want to hear this. I think of times when I was unhappy and sought solace by basking in my own despondency, secretly hoping that others would notice my downcast appearance and feel sorry for me. It's easy to revel in our own unhappiness. But this, in addition to being downright silly, is also cowardly.

It is easy to be unhappy. It takes no courage, no effort. Real worth comes from striving to be happy, from rejecting self-pity and the "feeling-good-feeling-bad" attitudes that bring misery to ourselves and others. We are at our best as human beings when we realize that happiness is largely under our control. Happiness is a choice to be made, not a feeling to be awaited. Great souls understand that they have no right to wallow in woe, because this makes others miserable. An unhappy parent places a heavy burden on any child. An unhappy child darkens the days of any parent. We have an obligation to ourselves and to others to strive for happiness.

Where to begin? With the realization that happiness comes at four levels: Happiness One, Happiness Two, Happiness Three, and Happiness Four. As we move up, we discover that each successive level is better because it is more enduring (lasts longer), because it is more pervasive (brings satisfaction at increasingly deeper levels of our being), and because it involves a fuller use of our human abilities (first body, next mind and will, then heart, then soul). And moving through the levels gives us a clearer understanding of the full meaning of happiness.

Paralleling the four levels of happiness are four levels of unhappiness, which (no surprise) may be characterized as Unhappiness One, Unhappiness Two, Unhappiness Three, and Unhappiness Four. We now examine each of these levels in turn.

HAPPINESS ONE

Happiness One is the pleasure we derive from the satisfaction of bodily appetites. We are hungry. We enjoy a fine meal, and that makes us happy. We are thirsty and find happiness in a cool drink. The satisfaction of any bodily appetite, including sexual desire, may be characterized as Happiness One.

Such happiness can be very intense. It brings immediate gratification. It requires no great intellectual activity. It exists primarily at the level of the body. But the satisfaction of bodily appetites, while intense, immediate, and obvious, has very real limitations.

I read somewhere about a gentleman who experienced such a limitation. He and his wife went to a new restaurant that served food buffet style. After they got their meals the owner inquired, "How's your dinner?" "Fine," the gentleman replied. "I enjoy buffets: I eat until my ankles hurt." "Until your ankles hurt?" asked the owner. "Yes," he said, "my wife kicks me under the table when I've had enough."

Bodily appetites have been placed in us by God for specific purposes. If we ignore these purposes, we will quickly discover Unhappiness One. Our appetite for food and drink is intended to help us nourish our bodies and maintain our health. If we use food to meet other needs, such as emotional ones, we can damage our health or be enmeshed in eating disorders like bulimia and anorexia. If we use alcohol to ease anxiety, we can end up in the gutter.

The satisfaction of bodily appetites is intense, but it is also short-lived. A few hours after a good meal, we are hungry again. This can lead to many kinds of addictions as we seek bodily pleasures that come and go quickly. We can become enslaved to cigarettes, alcohol, drugs, food, or sexual indulgence if we keep chasing after the high that all too soon becomes a low.

Even when there is no addiction, we can become bored with food, drink, or other bodily pleasures. We might enjoy pizza, but if pizza is served every meal for a week, we will lose our taste for it. For many reasons, then, Happiness One can lead to Unhappiness One. There must be more than the satisfaction of bodily appetites. And there is.

HAPPINESS TWO

Because of the limitations of Happiness One we must move beyond bodily pleasures to involve our mind and will. We do this by setting worthwhile goals and striving to achieve them. When we reach goals that require thought, decisions, and effort we move to the next level, Happiness Two, namely achievement, success, winning, the approval of others, self-esteem.

A child decides to play soccer. Her mind designs a plan; her will directs her body to work out and to practice. She makes the team—Happiness Two. A high-school student decides to become valedictorian. He resolves to pay attention in class, to spend long hours in study, to apply himself for four years. He graduates at the head of his class—Happiness Two. Adults work hard to provide a home and comfortable living for their family—Happiness Two.

But this level has limitations. First, if winning is the only way to happiness, most of us will be unhappy. Only one runner can win the gold medal, only one student can be valedictorian, only one team can take home the state championship. Second, winning doesn't guarantee lasting happiness. The luster of winning fades. Another race is run, another class graduates, another state championship is played. Last year's winners are forgotten. Third, making Happiness Two the center of our existence means that we depend on the approval of others to achieve satisfaction. We find ourselves at the mercy of public opinion, which can be a pitiless master, fickle and demanding. Fourth, putting Happiness Two first can distract us from more meaningful sources of joy, fixating us on possessions and leaving little time for family and friends. Finally, age has a way of turning winners into losers. The fastest runner slows. The most brilliant scholar grows forgetful. The rich and famous return to dust.

In these and many other ways, Happiness Two can become Unhappiness Two. If we wish to rise above this unhappiness, we must move past the struggle for achievement, success, and the approval of others. We must search for happiness on a higher level.

HAPPINESS THREE

We leave Unhappiness Two behind when we engage not only the body, mind, and will but also the heart. Instead of focusing on ourselves and our place in society, we consider the needs of others. Happiness Three occurs when we love and serve the neighbor. Here there is no competition. Acts of love and service benefit others and bring us deep and lasting joy.

Parents and grandparents find satisfaction and happiness in caring for their little ones. This is not the immediate gratification received from good food or a silver trophy, but a joy that is rich and deep. Jesus said, "There is more happiness in giving than in receiving" (see Acts 20:35), and parents who make sacrifices for their child realize the truth of his words. They experience joy in their child's first step, in hugs and kisses, in treasuring that child as a precious gift entrusted to them by God.

Sometimes they are rewarded with a good laugh. A friend told me she was driving granddaughter Chelsea, age nine, to a music lesson. Chelsea said earnestly, "Grandma, thanks so much for giving me a ride when I need to go someplace. When I'm sixteen and able to drive, I'll take you wherever you want to go…if you are still alive."

Soldiers in wartime who risk their lives to save a comrade, brothers on a fishing trip, friends enjoying lunch together, soccer teammates cheering one another, all experience Happiness Three. So do members of an organization dedicated to serving the poor, volunteer coaches of an elementary school volleyball squad, and blood donors. There really is more happiness in giving than in receiving.

But children become adults and leave home. Friends move to another state. A spouse grows old, then dies. Happiness Three becomes Unhappiness Three at every parting. There is a great deal of Unhappiness Three in every nursing home.

Unhappiness Three can also occur when people let us down. A grade-school buddy suddenly grows hostile. A teenage romance fades. A spouse allows love to fade away. An organization we hoped would change the world fails to make a difference. We discover that friends have faults, that good causes are flawed, and we slip into disillusionment and discouragement, Unhappiness Three.

A more subtle kind of Unhappiness Three arises when we expect friends and family to meet the deepest longings of our hearts. Even the best of friends and the truest human love cannot fill our need for perfect love, beauty, and truth. We have a hunger within us that nothing on earth can completely satisfy. There must be more.

HAPPINESS FOUR

"You have made us for yourself, O Lord, and our hearts are restless until they rest in you." Saint Augustine searched for happiness in sensual pleasures, in scholastic achievement, in worldly friendships, but these could not fulfill his deepest longings. Only when he rested in God could he find the happiness that satisfied his soul.

A little boy longs for Christmas and for the toy truck Santa will bring. He's sure it will make him perfectly happy. Christmas comes, and the toy, but not the perfect happiness. A figure skater expects that the Olympic gold medal will fulfill her every longing. The medal is placed around her neck and she finds herself wondering, "What will I do now?" A young woman is certain that marriage will fill her heart to the brim. Her husband is loving and generous, and their marriage is blessed with children. Years go by, and when she is told at her husband's funeral that they were fortunate to have had sixty years together, she can only whisper, "It was like a walk around the block." We do have longings that even the greatest earthly joys fail to meet. These longings point to a Reality capable of satisfying those longings, and that Reality is God.

Knowledge of God and friendship with God are Happiness Four. By faith we come to know God as a loving Father. We recognize Jesus Christ as the Lord and God who loved us even to death on a cross. We encounter the Holy Spirit as Guest of our souls. We find peace in God's promise to bring us through the limitations of this world, even death itself, to a happiness that will never fade.

Unhappiness Four is, of course, not knowing God. It's trying to find lasting happiness in the satisfaction of bodily appetites, in the chase after the approval of others, or even in devotion to people and good causes. Each level of happiness has its place, but only Happiness Four will give us the joy and peace we long for. When we understand the four levels of happiness and keep them in proper order, we can enjoy good food, accomplishments, friendship. Followers of Christ can be the happiest of human beings because they are taught by him to enjoy all God's gifts without mistaking them for the Giver. We can appreciate good food, the fun of competition, the satisfaction of helping others because these fit into a larger pattern of happiness, the pattern we find in the life and teachings of Jesus. In Jesus we find the resources to rise above unhappiness.

WHY UNHAPPINESS?

We were made by God to be happy. Why is there unhappiness? Human beings, according to the Bible, were created by God and set over a world that was "very good" (Genesis 1:31). They were made "in the image of God" (Genesis 1:27), an expression denoting their ability to know and love. They were given also the freedom to make choices, for without freedom love is impossible.

The first man and woman, named Adam and Eve in Scripture, were meant to enjoy happiness at every level. Happiness One: Their home was a garden of Eden, a paradise, where plants were "good for food" (Genesis 2:9). Happiness Two: They were given dominion over "every living thing" (Genesis 1:28). Happiness Three: So great was their union of body and spirit that Adam described Eve as "bone of my bones and flesh of my flesh" (Genesis 2:23). Happiness Four: Adam and Eve enjoyed such intimacy with their Creator that God was portrayed walking in the garden, searching for them (Genesis 3:8).

But happiness for Adam and Eve depended on their recognizing God as the source and goal of life, and on freely choosing to know, love, and obey God. The author of Genesis, with brilliant insight, depicts this reality by stating that God had planted in the garden a tree of the knowledge of good and evil. This tree represented God's wisdom in designating what was good for human beings (virtue) and what was evil (sin). Obeying God would bring happiness. Disobeying God would bring grief. Satan, a spirit who had rebelled against God, convinced Adam and Eve that God had no right to decree what was good or bad. They could decide for themselves and "be like God, knowing good and evil" (Genesis 3:5). They foolishly believed Satan. They rejected God in an act of defiance, the original sin, symbolized by their eating of the tree of the knowledge of good and evil.

Instantly their world turned upside down. In God's plan, they had been meant to honor God's primacy, love one another, enjoy success, and savor bodily pleasures. Now honor became fear as they hid from God. Love changed to hostility as they blamed each other for their folly. Success would henceforth involve struggle and be entangled with the thorns and thistles of disordered egos. The satisfaction of bodily appetites would come only with toil. Pleasure would cost pain, sweat, blood, the pangs of childbearing, and a final return to dust. The garden of Eden had become a vale of tears (Genesis 3:8–24).

Their first impulse was no longer the pursuit of Happiness Four and Three, love of God and one another. Instead, Happiness One took precedence as they sought to satisfy disorderly appetites for food, drink, and sex. Happiness Two turned into the desire to dominate, as those who had been partners (Genesis 2:20) became ruler and ruled (Genesis 3:16). Happiness Three and Four slipped into the background.

Sadly, because Adam and Eve were parents of the whole of humanity, their sin affected the human nature transmitted to their descendants. The Bible shows the effects of sin in the murder of Abel by his brother Cain, and in the web of evil that clings to humanity throughout history. We see these effects today in our imperfect human condition, in the way unruly appetites cause destruction. A truck driver with an alcohol blood level twice the legal limit crosses a highway center line and kills eight college students. A popular singer, afflicted with bulimia, starves herself to death. A respected judge is arrested for murdering his wife in order to marry a younger woman. Fabulously wealthy athletes sulk and destroy team unity because they feel unappreciated.

The effects of the sin of our first parents are not always so drastic. Sometimes they can be humorous. A little boy was visiting his grandmother, who happened to be baking chocolate chip cookies. She placed a plateful before him, and he promptly gobbled them down. She handed him a few more, and soon noticed a strange look on his face. "What's the matter, Timmy?" she asked. "Don't you want any more cookies?" "No," he replied, "I don't even want the ones I already ate." But even in the humor, we detect the disorder of appetites that do not easily accept control.

If we are to enjoy happiness at every level and keep it from dissolving into unhappiness, we must address the damage done by Adam and Eve. This means we must accept the order established by God at creation.

RESTORING ORDER

We could not restore the relationship of love between God and creature that existed before the sin of Adam and Eve. Only God could do that by forgiving us. Only God could rebuild the bridge of love and trust that we had foolishly destroyed. And God, with infinite love and mercy, reached out to fallen humanity by entering into our world. God became one of us in Jesus Christ. Jesus as God could forgive our sins. Jesus as one of us could offer a life of perfect love that would restore the unity between us and God lost by our first parents. His death, the greatest act of love in history, brought forgiveness and reunion with God: "No one has greater love than this, to lay down one's life for one's friends" (John 15:13).

In the Garden of Eden, God called out to Adam and Eve, "Where are you?" They had, after sinning, hidden themselves out of fear, then compounded their troubles by making lame excuses. In Jesus Christ, God calls out to us again. We answer with a joyful "Here I am." We accept the priorities God has established, turning away from sin and putting our faith in Christ, who alone can save us from the power of evil. We express our faith in everyday life, striving to think, speak, and act as Jesus did. No longer hiding from God, we invite Father, Son, and Holy Spirit into our hearts.

Soon after the death and Resurrection of Jesus, Peter preached the news of God's desire to save us through Jesus Christ. Peter's listeners were touched and asked what to do. Peter said, "Repent, and be baptized every one of you in the name of Jesus Christ so that your sins may be forgiven; and you will receive the gift of the Holy Spirit" (Acts 2:38). This acceptance of Jesus Christ and his message of salvation brought happiness to believers, not just at prayer, but in every circumstance of life. Getting things right with God even brought new joy to the satisfaction of bodily appetites as they "broke bread at home and ate their food with glad and generous hearts" (Acts 2:46).

Getting things right with God, putting things in proper order, can bring new joy to us when we learn to appreciate physical pleasure as God intends. We find God's order of things in the Church, the community of believers established by Christ. We discover God's plan for our happiness in the Scriptures God inspired.

The Ten Commandments, for example, can be viewed in many ways. Here we see them as God-given guidelines to lead us to the happiness God wants for us. The commandments tell us what to do in order to enjoy Happiness One, Two, Three and Four. They tell us what to avoid in order to escape Unhappiness One, Two, Three and Four. In the commandments and elsewhere in Scripture, as understood in the community of the Church, we will find practical patterns for happy living.

LIVING THE FOUR LEVELS

When I think of happiness and recall really happy individuals I've known, I remember Lon, who spent his whole life in southeast Missouri. Lon was a simple man of great faith who loved his wife and their ten children. After 53 years of marriage, Lon's wife died. Some years later at the age of 84, Lon married Myrtle, a widow ten years younger. Friends smiled and said Lon was looking for someone to watch over him in old age. But less than a year later, Myrtle suffered a stroke. Lon cared for her at home for several years. Eventually, she had to go to a nursing home. For five years, until she died, Lon visited her daily, walking the quarter mile from his house to the nursing home, where he stayed with her for hours at a time. He never complained. He loved Myrtle "in sickness and in health." He accepted what God gave, and gave with a smile what God asked.

After Myrtle died, Lon remained active and in touch with those he loved. One afternoon I visited him, now in his mid nineties, at the home of his grandson. Lon was playing cards with members of his family. He had a cold beer at his right hand and the ever-present smile on his face. Recalling the scene, I recognize the four levels of happiness. Happiness One was the cold beer. Happiness Two was the competition of the card game (which Lon played very well). Happiness Three was being with family and friends. Happiness Four was Lon's deep faith in God, assuring him that the joys of this life were but a foretaste of those to come.

Lon knew the answer to the question, "Why did God make you?" Lon spent his life getting to know God through prayer and frequent attendance at Mass. He found God in the ordinary pleasures of life and in the rewards of supporting his family. He found God in those he loved. And when Lon died at the age of 101, I'm sure he saw his God face to face.

Lon knew God made us to be happy. But he also knew that God does not make us happy. We must work at that. If we understand the four levels of happiness and build our lives on a proper understanding of them, we will find happiness. In the next four chapters, we will examine the four levels in detail. We will see how we can attain each level of happiness and avoid each level of unhappiness. We will examine the life and teaching of Jesus a model and path to happiness. In this, as in all things, Jesus is our way, our truth, and our life.

REFLECTIONS

Have the four levels helped you to understand happiness in a new way? Now that you have read this Introduction, can you create a definition of happiness based on the four levels? What are your most memorable experiences of Happiness One, Two, Three, and Four during the past year? Of Unhappiness One, Two, Three, and Four? As you look back over your life, can you think of situations where you experienced all four levels of happiness together? Can you name some truly happy people, like Lon, who helped you to appreciate the meaning of happiness? Have you ever considered how much God desires happiness for you? Do you view keeping the commandments and practicing your faith as the best pathways to happiness?

ONE

BODY

Pleasure's Rewards and Limits

F rank's hobby is Italian cooking, and he is a master at it. He purchases the finest ingredients from a family grocery on the Hill in Saint Louis, Missouri. Herbs and spices come from his own garden. As he prepares a meal, the kitchen is filled with the fragrances of bread baking, simmering sauces, freshly grated Parmesan cheese, Italian sausage, herbs and spices. Frank samples the various courses, adding a bit of this or that until he's sure each dish is just right. Soon family and friends gather at table, and to the enjoyment of delightful aromas is added the pleasure of sampling flavors that definitely qualify as Happiness One.

JESUS, THE BIBLE, AND HAPPINESS ONE

If we enjoy food and drink, we are in the best of company, Jesus himself. When wine ran out at a wedding party, Jesus worked a miracle to provide vintage of the highest quality (John 2:1–11). He miraculously multiplied bread and fish to feed a hungry crowd (Mark 6:35–44). He prepared breakfast for his apostles, baking bread and grilling fish for them (John 21:9–12). In contrast to John the Baptist, who was renowned for his austerity, Jesus enjoyed food and wine so much that he was criticized by his enemies (Luke 7:34). He even used the symbolism of a banquet to foreshadow the happiness of heaven (Matthew 22:2).

The Jewish Scriptures taught that appetites for food and drink came from God. At the Creation, God said to the first man and woman, "See, I have given you every plant yielding seed that is upon the face of all the earth, and every tree with seed in its fruit; you shall have them for food" (Genesis 1:29).

When the Jews wanted to describe an idyllic period in their history, they spoke of it in terms of Happiness One. "Judah and Israel were as numerous as the sand by the sea; they ate and drank and were happy" (1 Kings 4:20). The Jews saw food and drink as among the choicest of God's blessings. They were grateful that God had given "wine to gladden the human heart, / oil to make the face shine, / and bread to strengthen the human heart" (Psalm 104:15).

The Scriptures speak highly of sexual pleasure. After all, sex was God's idea: "So God created humankind in his image, / in the image of God he created them; / male and female he created them" (Genesis 1:27). Many Old Testament books, like Ruth and Tobit, praise the goodness of marital love. The Song of Solomon and prophetic works like Jeremiah and Hosea use the romance and passion of human love to describe God's love for us. So does Paul in the New Testament: "'For this reason a man will leave his father and mother and be joined to his wife, and the two will become one flesh.' This is a great mystery, and I am applying it to Christ and the church" (Ephesians 5:31–32).

THE BIBLE AND UNHAPPINESS ONE

Natalie, age three, loved butter. When no one was looking, she would grasp a stick of butter and try to eat it like a Popsicle. No matter how many times her parents took it away, they couldn't convince her that it wasn't good for her. One day her father saw her sitting on the floor gorging herself from a tub of margarine. In desperation he sat her on a chair and put the tub in front of her. "Go ahead," he said. "Eat as much as you want." Natalie couldn't believe her good fortune. What had been forbidden was now within her grasp. She ate and ate. Like Adam and Eve, however, she soon learned that forbidden food has a very serious downside. For our first parents, it was expulsion from the Garden. For Natalie, it was a stomachache that cured her forever of her craving for butter.

Happiness One, the satisfaction of bodily appetites for food, drink, and sexual pleasure, is seen as good in the Judeo-Christian tradition. But it is not an unrestricted good. The Bible warns against excess. "Do not be greedy for every delicacy, and do not eat without restraint; for overeating brings sickness, and gluttony leads to nausea" (Sirach 37:29–30).

Jesus says: "Be on your guard so that your hearts are not weighed down with dissipation and drunkenness" (Luke 21:34). Paul advises us to "live honorably as in the day, not in reveling and drunkenness, not in debauchery and licentiousness" (Romans 13:13). There are many reasons why the Bible cautions restraint in dealing with bodily appetites. Some are implied in the passages just quoted. Unrestrained enjoyment of food and wine can lead to gluttony and drunkenness. Love can be swallowed up by lust. Happiness One then becomes Unhappiness One.

We've already seen that satisfying bodily appetites can produce intense pleasure. It brings immediate gratification and requires no training or serious thought. The intensity comes from the primitive nature of our drives for survival and reproduction. If these drives are allowed free rein, they can lead to the foulest treacheries and to personal catastrophe.

Even the high and mighty can be dragged into the depths of unhappiness by the attractions of physical pleasure. King David saw Bathsheba bathing and was swept away by her beauty. He committed adultery, then murdered her husband, Uriah, one of his most loyal soldiers (2 Samuel 11—12). Another dramatic example of how quickly Happiness One can generate unhappiness is the story of David's son, Amnon. Amnon became infatuated with his half sister, Tamar. He feigned illness to have her visit him, then raped her, disdaining her pitiful pleas for mercy. "No, my brother, do not force me; for such a thing is not done in Israel; do not do anything so vile! As for me, where could I carry my shame?" (2 Samuel 13:12–13).

Amnon had his way with Tamar. But inordinate pleasure can quickly turn to disgust. "Then Amnon was seized with a very great loathing for her; indeed, his loathing was even greater than the lust he had felt for her. Amnon said to her, 'Get out!' But she said to him, 'No, my brother; for this wrong in sending me away is greater than the other that you did to me.' But he would not listen to her" (2 Samuel 13:15–16).

David's lust set a pattern followed by his children. Amnon's lust led to his murder at the hands of Tamar's vengeful brother, Absalom. History is full of stories like those of David and Amnon. Our own day has seen its share of tragedies involving political, military, educational, and religious leaders who let lust lead them down a path to shame and self-destruction.

How can something that seems so good be so bad? How can something that seems so right be so wrong? These questions are asked by many who cannot see beyond Happiness One or realize its limitations. The limitations are rooted in the disorder of original sin, as explained in the Introduction.

The order that would have resulted in unending happiness for humanity—God first, then people, achievement, and pleasure—was reversed by the sin of Adam and Eve. Pleasure seized the first place, and the power of human urges for survival and reproduction can easily push God, reason, and achievement into the background. Perhaps this is why the author of Genesis chose the act of eating to symbolize the first sin. He saw how often human beings are drawn from God to the pursuit of pleasure. He knew that the overturning of priorities set by God inevitably leads to unhappiness. We need to regain those priorities.

STEPS TOWARD HAPPINESS ONE

To enjoy Happiness One we must first realize that God has designed bodily appetites for specific purposes. Food and drink are to nourish our body and give pleasure. Misused, they cause harm. "Happy are you, O land...when your princes feast at the proper time— / for strength, and not for drunkenness!" (Ecclesiastes 10:17). Recent research has reinforced this ancient advice. Wine in moderation, for example, can significantly lower the risk of heart disease. Excessive use of alcohol, on the contrary, does a great deal of damage.

Any use of food or drink that is hurtful to ourselves or others is disordered. Sexual pleasure is intended for marriage as an expression of faithful, committed love (Genesis 2:24; Mark 10:6–12). God's commandments reinforce these directives. The commandment "You shall not kill" includes care for the life God gave us, and we must not kill ourselves with food or drink. The commandments "You shall not commit adultery, You shall not covet your neighbor's wife" teach that sexual pleasure has limits.

We must learn to subject bodily appetites to our mind and will. This takes reflection and resolve. Bodily appetites are powerful and undisciplined. They are accelerated by modern advertising and the media, which encourage us to surrender to every urge. If we wait for temptation to strike before we set our priorities, we are doomed to failure. Perhaps David would have controlled his desires if he had previously considered the wickedness of adultery and murder. Today those who want to control their sexual urges must consider the evils that can flow from hedonism. Movies and television would have us believe that sexual pleasure brings unlimited satisfaction and does no harm.

The dangers of promiscuity are seldom mentioned. Nor are the tragedies that spring from loss of self-control: broken homes, abused children, battered women, disease, and psychological trauma.

We must also spend time reflecting on the words and example of Jesus, who encourages us to love with purity and holiness. We must realize that we rise above the animals when we control immoderate urges. I once spoke to a man whose wife became seriously ill shortly after their marriage. For seven years sexual intercourse was impossible. He said, "It wasn't difficult to be faithful. I loved her so much that I couldn't imagine hurting her by adultery." Real strength and heroism are found in this kind of fidelity, not in the casual sex glorified in the media.

We must avoid unnecessary temptations and stay out of compromising situations. Someone forbidden by the doctor to eat doughnuts should not enter the bakery. We cannot be chaste if we bury our minds in pornography. Temptations no longer reside exclusively in the seedy part of town. They are as close as the click of a remote switch or a keyword on the Internet. The purveyors of pornography claim that it is harmless, that no one is hurt. The reality is very different. Victims are everywhere. Those who sell their own bodies, women and children devalued into sex objects, those whose values are debased by pornography, families that are divided—these and many others are victims. Pornography comes from the deepest part of hell, and it never loses the stench of its origins.

We must realize also that as lust begins to take over a person, reason departs. Satan slithers in with the suggestion that, after all, the body is beautiful and God's commandments are old-fashioned: "What does God know about good and evil?" The forbidden fruit of immoral pleasure becomes attractive. A temptation that could easily have been controlled at the beginning takes hold and becomes irresistible. A moment's pleasure seems to outweigh all else. When hormones override the brain, terrible decisions and grave unhappiness result.

Some people have a genetic predisposition to addictions of various kinds, to alcohol, drugs, food, sexual pleasure. Often this condition results in a serious loss of control over one's capability to function in society. Alcoholics, for example, can quickly destroy themselves and bring misery to their families. Such people need professional help or the assistance of a group like Alcoholics Anonymous. AA has had much success in helping alcoholics recover, and it is worth noting that this and similar self-help groups begin with the importance of redesigning one's life into a pattern that puts God first.

Those who want to stay free of addictive substances should learn to appreciate the nonaddictive joys of life. One beautiful summer afternoon, after a delicious lunch at an outdoor café in Aspen, Colorado, I was walking with friends Pat and Sheila along a mountain path. Birds chirped in the forest and a stream murmured gently. Soft breezes ruffled green aspen leaves against a background of snow-topped peaks and clear blue sky. Pat remarked, "It's incredible that people have to use cocaine to get high."

We can enrich our ability to enjoy Happiness One by integrating it with the other levels of happiness. Kathy does this by celebrating holidays in a big way. At Easter the dining room is full of flowers and candles and brightly colored eggs. Tablecloth and napkins and napkin holders have a springtime theme. The traditional Easter ham is surrounded by delicacies of every kind. Everything sings Resurrection and new life. At Thanksgiving there are fall flowers and symbols of the harvest: turkey and dressing, pumpkin pie and pecan pie and apple pie, and several kinds of wine. Family and friends gather around the table and prayers are said. Happiness One is enhanced by Happiness Two (justifiable pride in presenting a banquet worthy of the occasion), Happiness Three (the love of family and friends), and Happiness Four (prayer and celebrating God's goodness at Easter, at Thanksgiving, and always). "So, whether you eat or drink, or whatever you do, do everything for the glory of God" (1 Corinthians 10:31).

APPRECIATING HAPPINESS ONE

While we should be aware of the power of bodily appetites to override reason and cause harm, we ought not be negative toward them. Appetites for food, drink, and pleasure are gifts of God and are to be appreciated. One way of growing in such appreciation is to be aware of how good habits of eating and drinking can enhance health and well-being, thereby helping us to succeed, perform works of charity, and serve God.

We should also notice how Happiness One is associated with important moments in life, moments linked to Happiness Two, Three, and Four. Food and drink add enjoyment to attendance at athletic contests. Hot dogs and cold drinks go well with home runs, touchdowns, goals, and points scored. Intermissions bring long lines to food stands. High schools and colleges schedule banquets to honor most valuable players and most improved performers.

We take it for granted that family events will be celebrated with meals. Birthday cakes show our appreciation for the lives of those we love. Weddings and anniversaries are made even more special by meals memorable for fine food and toasts to the bride and groom. Sometimes even a simple celebration can produce unforgettable moments of Happiness Three. I once read about a young couple invited for ice cream and cake at the home of their neighbors who were observing their fifty-second wedding anniversary. The younger man remarked, "Fifty-two years. That's a long time with one person." The elderly gentleman put his arm around his wife, smiled, and replied, "It would have been a whole lot longer without her."

The Jewish people recall how God freed them from slavery in Egypt at their annual Passover meal of roasted lamb, unleavened bread, wine, and herbs. Jesus celebrated his Last Supper at a Passover meal with his apostles, and then told his followers to remember him always by repeating what he did until the end of time.

My life as a priest has been blessed with Happiness Four, and it has been marked with fun and good food at countless parish dinners. At my twenty-fifth anniversary of ordination to the priesthood, St. Denis Parish in Benton, Missouri, observed the occasion with a wonderful meal and humorous gifts. The most memorable of these was a toy car decorated with a set of antlers, recalling a sudden encounter I'd had the previous year with an unfortunate deer on Interstate 55.

The more we understand how food and drink can be part of a happy life when used in accord with God's plan, the better we'll be able to appreciate these blessings. With such an appreciation, we are more likely to use food and drink well, and to fit any kind of physical pleasure into God's design for our happiness.

FASTING

Strange as it may seem, fasting can be an important element in our goal of enjoying happiness to the fullest. Fasting is mentioned frequently in the Old Testament (for example, Judith 8:6; 2 Chronicles 20:3; Joel 1:14). Jesus fasted (Matthew 4:2) and counseled fasting for his followers (Matthew 6:16). Fasting from food and drink can express sorrow for sin and thereby help us redirect our life's priorities according to those established by God. By fasting we imitate Jesus, who in the desert reversed the direction taken by Adam and Eve in the Garden of Eden. They rejected God and listened to Satan. Jesus rejected Satan and followed God's word. Adam and Eve disobeyed the word of God and ate the forbidden fruit. Jesus affirmed that we cannot live "by bread alone, but by every word that comes from the mouth of God" (Matthew 4:4).

Members of the early Church fasted and prayed to seek God's guidance (Acts 13:3). So fasting is appropriate when we are searching for direction from God in a difficult decision or when we are praying for a significant need. Fasting can help control unruly desires for immediate gratification and guide us to sources of happiness that run long and deep.

Fasting can make our spiritual senses more alert. A hunger for food reminds us of those people throughout the world who do not have enough to eat, and prompts us to find joy in helping them. Fasting from food and drink gives us a feeling of hunger, of emptiness. This should recall our far more significant hunger for God, and the emptiness to be filled with the joy only God can supply.

How we fast depends on many factors, including age, health, family concerns, and the demands of work. Some people go an entire day without taking any solid food. (Anyone abstaining from food should drink plenty of liquids.) Others omit breakfast or lunch, or cut back significantly at these meals. Some individuals fast from television, secular reading, or other entertainments.

What is most important is not the negative aspect of fasting, but the positive elements of redirection to works of charity for the neighbor and devotion to God. I read about a pastor who announced to his congregation that as an act of communal penance for Lent, the parish would not heat the church building until Easter. As he greeted the church members after the service, he asked an elderly parishioner, "And Mrs. White, what will you be giving up for Lent?" She looked right at him and replied, "Church." That, of course, would not be a step forward. Fasting which leads us closer to God and neighbor is a holy discipline that will bring happiness as well.

MOVING ON TO THE NEXT LEVELS

After their marriage back in the 1960s, Ben and Kay lived on a military base while Ben learned to fly helicopters. They didn't have a car, and an officer made his automobile available for Ben and Kay so they could bring their newborn daughter to the doctor for checkups. To express their gratitude, they bought a bottle of rum for the officer. Ben delivered it and was invited in for a rum and cola. Ben had never tried rum and had limited experience with any kind of alcoholic beverage. The first drink tasted fine, and the officer poured another, and another. When Ben finally arrived back home, he could only crawl on his hands and knees to the bathroom where he hung his head into the commode and deposited what he had been drinking. Kay was furious, stormed into the bathroom, and slammed the cover down on Ben's head. He woke up a few hours later with a very bad headache and a new appreciation for the power of rum and cola to produce unhappiness.

Forty years later, Ben and Kay still laugh about this misadventure. They enjoy food and drink (Happiness One), more so because there's never been a similar incident. Ben wanted to be a pilot, to achieve success in a very difficult field (Happiness Two), and this desire helped him keep appetites in check. Ben and Kay love each other dearly (Happiness Three), and they were able to work through the rum and cola incident because of that love. They have a deep faith in God and they've always looked to God for guidance and strength (Happiness Four).

Like them, we enjoy Happiness One, and move on to the next levels.

REFLECTIONS

Jesus enjoyed food and drink. How many instances of this can you recall from the New Testament? Natalie learned to control her appetite for butter when she had too much of a good thing. Have you had similar experiences? In what ways do modern advertising and the media lead people astray by making Happiness One promise more than it can deliver? This chapter states that those who want to stay free of addictions should learn to appreciate the nonaddictive joys of life. What are your favorite nonaddictive joys? How can these be seen as gifts of God? Meals are often connected to events that qualify as Happiness Two, Three, and Four. Can you think of examples in your own life? How important is fasting to you? Has reading this chapter helped you to see it in a new way?

TWO

MIND AND WILL
Winning and Losing

P eople love to compete. Two young brothers, shouting and
laughing, race down the sidewalk to see who can reach
home first. Four elderly gentlemen play cards all morning.
Six-year-old Kristen makes her dad throw batting practice until
his arm hurts. Olympic athletes stage their games before the world.

Go to any county fair, and you'll see that competition is not
limited to games and sports. Ethel hopes her grape jelly will win
a blue ribbon. Timmy dreams that his prize lamb will be named
best in show. There are ribbons for baked goods, metalwork,
carpentry, arts and crafts. People love the challenge of putting
forth their finest efforts and weighing the results against the best
others can do.

Such competition seems ingrained in human nature. The reasons for this are interesting and complex. Sporting contests in-
vigorate our bodies. The processes of winning and losing can help
us mature emotionally. Card and board games sharpen our memo-
ries, test our minds, and strengthen our wills. Competitions of
every kind allow children and adults to assess their talents and
reinforce abilities necessary for success in school, work, and social life.

Happiness Two does not always require competition. The
satisfaction of completing a difficult project at work or school is
Happiness Two. So is the sense of accomplishment parents experi-

ence in providing a home for their family. The elation felt at making a quilt, finishing a painting, cleaning the house, decorating for Christmas, and achieving many other goals is Happiness Two.

BETTER THAN HAPPINESS ONE

Happiness Two takes us a step above Happiness One. We go beyond bodily pleasure and involve mind and will. In those areas which distinguish the four levels from one another, Happiness Two surpasses Happiness One in duration, pervasiveness, and involvement of our human abilities.

Duration: The happiness that comes from satisfying bodily appetites passes quickly. Happiness Two lasts longer. High-school athletes smile each time they pass the display case with its trophy for last year's state championship. Physicians display in their offices the diplomas that mark their progress through medical school and certify their qualifications to perform their duties. Homeowners take great satisfaction in maintaining and improving their property.

Pervasiveness: Gratifying bodily appetites makes us feel good on a physical level, but Happiness Two can touch body, emotions, and mind. A skilled athlete standing on the winner's podium feels the pleasurable fatigue of a gold-medal effort, the joy experienced at doing one's best, and the satisfaction of having followed a well-planned training regimen. A valedictorian speaks at graduation, her mind finely tuned, her will strengthened by hard work, her emotions rewarded in the applause of faculty, students, and parents.

Involvement of human abilities: There's little skill needed to swallow down a meal, but Happiness Two requires training of the body, control of the emotions, sharpening of the mind, and resolve in the will. Here we move into areas that are specific to human beings. Animals do not schedule training sessions in order to prepare for a race. Animals do not study for exams in physics. Human beings do. We rise to the challenges of being human when we strive for success. As a result, Happiness Two is richer and deeper than Happiness One.

Amy was a good student in high school and a determined runner. She studied hard and ranked near the top of her class. She did not possess exceptional speed, but accepted the guidance of her coach and trained rigorously. She helped her team win the state cross-country championship her senior year. Some college coaches did not think Amy could compete successfully at the next level, but one who was aware of her intelligence and determination offered her a scholarship. In college Amy used her mind to set goals, to prepare a training program, select healthful food, and achieve academic excellence. She used her will to discipline herself for the discomfort of long, hard training runs and difficult races against strong competition. As a result, she not only competed but won often, and in her sophomore year Amy was named conference runner of the year.

There are people with a great deal of talent who fail to achieve much because they allow bodily cravings for food, drink, and slumber to dull their abilities. Success comes to those who, like Amy, let mind and will take charge of the body. In the satisfaction of exercising our abilities to know and decide, we reach worthwhile goals. We find Happiness Two.

SCRIPTURE AND HAPPINESS TWO

Our desire to do well may be rooted in the fact that we are made in the image and likeness of God. God competes with no one. But when God does something, it is done perfectly. The universe God created is, as the Book of Genesis notes, "very good." When Jesus changed water into wine at the wedding feast of Cana, he was not content to produce a merely passable vintage. His wine was the best (John 2:1–11). Psalm 118 praises God for marvelous works of salvation and asks: "O Lord, we beseech you, give us success" (25). Psalm 90 compares the greatness of God with our own human weaknesses, then prays: "O prosper the work of our hands" (17). It is as if the psalmist wants God's power, success, and prosperity to flow into us. When we do well, we imitate God.

Competition, striving, and winning find their way into Scripture. There is an amusing detail in John's description of Christ's Resurrection. Mary Magdalene related to Peter and another disciple that Christ's tomb was empty. Peter and the other disciple, probably the author of John's Gospel, "were running together, but the other disciple outran Peter and reached the tomb first" (John 20:4). It's almost as if John couldn't resist adding the detail that he was the faster runner.

Saint Paul uses the language of competitive sports. To him, winning is important. "Do you not know that in a race the runners all compete, but only one receives the prize? Run in such a way that you may win it. Athletes exercise self-control in all things; they do it to receive a perishable wreath, but we an imperishable one. So I do not run aimlessly, nor do I box as though beating the air; but I punish my body and enslave it, so that after proclaiming to others I myself should not be disqualified" (1 Corinthians 9:24–27).

SCRIPTURE AND UNHAPPINESS TWO

Happiness Two, the joy that comes from success, from accomplishment, from winning, is a good thing. But it has limitations, mentioned in the Introduction, that can be found throughout Scripture. The first limitation is that winners presuppose losers.

Saint Paul observes that many runners compete in a race, but only one wins the prize. Second, while Happiness Two does go beyond the gratification of bodily appetites, it cannot satisfy our deepest human longings. The Book of Ecclesiastes portrays Solomon as a king who had achieved at the highest level, then derided his accomplishments as "vanity and chasing after wind" (Ecclesiastes 2:11; 4:16). Third, much of the satisfaction gained from Happiness Two depends on recognition from others. Such recognition does not last. David defeated Goliath and won acclaim from King Saul. All too soon Saul did his best to kill David. Fourth, the pursuit of wealth and status symbols can easily distract us from the more important things in life, as Jesus shows in parables like the story of the rich man and Lazarus (Luke 16:19–31). Finally, age gradually brings to a halt our ability to succeed in the eyes of the world. Death ends competition, and the hard-earned trophies of wealth must be left behind. "So I turned and gave my heart up to despair concerning all the toil of my labors under the sun, because sometimes one who has toiled with wisdom and knowledge and skill must leave all to be enjoyed by another who did not toil for it" (Ecclesiastes 2:20–21). The psalmist bewails the shortness of life and human endeavor, for "...our years come to an end like a sigh. / The days of our life are seventy years, / or perhaps eighty, if we are strong; / even then their span is only toil and trouble; / they are soon gone, and we fly away" (Psalm 90:9–10).

UNHAPPINESS TWO TODAY

In today's world it is far too easy to ignore the wisdom of Scripture and the lessons of human experience. If only one runner can win the race, there should be no disgrace for the others. Yet we hear, "Winning isn't everything. It's the only thing." Where this attitude prevails, winners become arrogant and losers grow depressed.

Feelings of superiority and inferiority produce alienation. People who believe that winning is the only thing do anything to win. Athletes cheat, break the rules, deliberately injure others, damage their own bodies with drugs. Coaches scream at small children for dropping a fly ball or fumbling a punt. Parents curse coaches and fight one another. I read somewhere that a Little League coach said to one of his players, "We don't believe in temper tantrums, screaming at umpires, using bad language, or sulking when we lose. Do you understand?" The boy nodded yes. "All right, then," the coach went on, "Do you think you can explain that to your father jumping around over there in the stands?"

The fact that success, achievement, acclaim, and wealth do not guarantee happiness can be shown by a glance through the daily newspaper or a search on the Internet. One day's sports news recently contained stories about a National Football league player arrested for domestic violence, a hockey star charged with felony drug possession, a boxer sent to prison for an assault on his girlfriend, a college football kicker accused of attempted bribery, and a National League baseball pitcher arrested for beating his wife and holding a gun to her head in front of their two-year-old son. Achievement in other high profile areas doesn't equate with happiness either. A Hollywood columnist wrote that Hollywood movie stars exist for one reason: to show the rest of us that no amount of money, fame, or pleasure will bring lasting happiness.

Fame is as fleeting and fickle today as it was in biblical times. Athletes and actors, singers and artists win acclaim and are soon forgotten. Even the most powerful of political leaders can be swept away on the changing tide of public opinion. After the Gulf War, President George Bush, Sr., had some of the highest approval ratings ever recorded. But by the next presidential election he had already fallen out of favor and was defeated. That Happiness Two comes with time limits is no surprise to any small town high-school athlete. A few years after he graduates his trophies are tarnished, and he has learned that there are better ways to begin a conversation than, "Did I ever tell you about the game when I ran for two hundred yards and scored four touchdowns?"

Harry Chapin's folk song, "The Cat's in the Cradle," describes a father so intent on making money that he had no time for his son, who idolized his dad and wanted to be just like him. When the father grew old and needed the son's attention, he discovered that the young man had grown up just like him—too busy chasing success to care about people. (Album, *Verities & Balderdash*, 1974. Lyrics by Sandra Chapin.)

Focusing overmuch on Happiness Two, on having the largest house on the block, on driving the most expensive car in town, often separates parents from children and deprives both of higher levels of happiness. I once listened to a mother describe the problems that her children, raised in wealth and privilege, were experiencing with drugs and personality disorders. She ended with the words, "I wish we'd never had all that money."

The passing of years and the inevitability of death are no less sure for us than they were for the great ones of the Old Testament. Renowned tenors lose their voice. Dancers slow to a shuffle. Athletes retire. Aging professors leave the classroom, never to return. The names of the rich, the famous, and the mighty make the news one final time—in the obituaries. If Happiness Two was their primary goal in life, death can only be a tragedy. And tragedy it is if one's last thought must be: "I'm dying with plenty of money in the bank, or trophies on the shelf, or victims in my wake."

ROOTS OF UNHAPPINESS TWO

Why are we drawn into the quest for acclaim, wealth, and success the way a moth is drawn to the flame? The sin of Adam and Eve caused the same distortion in our pursuit of achievement as in our search for pleasure. Just as rebellious bodily appetites can overthrow the rule of reason and common sense, so too can unruly needs for praise and acclaim. We are out of balance. Adam first saw Eve as his partner. After their sin, he viewed himself as ruler and Eve as ruled. Competition and domination became his primary way of relating to others. It was the same with Cain, who killed his brother Abel because Cain could not tolerate being second-best. This defect of character has been passed down to us.

Barbara told me about a high-school classmate of hers who used to check the labels on dresses and blouses others were wearing, then ridicule the girls who were not attired in designer clothing. This kind of pitiless pride, which kills the spirits of innocent victims, mimics the crime of Abel with its terrible need to exalt oneself by punishing others.

The sin of Adam and Eve continues to haunt us. More proximately, our sometimes desperate chase after approval may be rooted in the insecurities we experience in our imperfect world. A child growing up in a home where praise is seldom given is likely to hunger for approval as an adult. But children too often praised can become addicted to flattery. How do we find a balance? How can we experience Happiness Two without sinking into Unhappiness?

STRIVING FOR HAPPINESS TWO

We must seek out the priorities established by God at the beginning. Instead of hiding from God, we must look to God as the solid foundation for our sense of self-worth. Paradoxically, we find our own great value when we acknowledge the primacy of God.

God is perfect, and God's power and wisdom are without limits. God can do only what is best, because God is the measure of all that is. So when God chose to be a human being, God showed us what is worthwhile in human existence. God showed us who is of value.

Jesus could have been born in a palace at Rome. He could have been born in our day and become so great a golfer that he'd make Tiger Woods look like a duffer. Instead, he chose to be born of humble parents in a stable at Bethlehem. He lived in a small town and worked at ordinary manual labor. Since God cannot do what is second-best, this must mean that a common life, the kind of life within the reach of any human being, is the pinnacle of human achievement.

Many of us may look in the mirror and consider: "I'll never appear on the cover of *Time*. I'll never make as much money as Bill Gates. I'm just a nobody." That's not what God thinks. In God's estimation, the kind of life we lead as ordinary people is so important that God incarnate, Jesus Christ, could not find a better way to spend the first thirty years of his human existence than to be like us. He got up in the morning, prayed, ate, worked in the carpenter shop, and generally lived in such ordinary fashion that his neighbors thought he was nobody special (Mark 6:1–6). Our value comes not from human opinion, which is both fickle and fallible, but from the esteem of God. And God makes it clear that ordinary people and ordinary lives are precious. As Abraham Lincoln said, "God must love common people. He made so many of them."

Even more important, God views us as beloved children. Jesus taught us to call God our Father. Saint Paul addressed the Corinthians, and us, as sons and daughters of God (2 Corinthians 6:18). Prayer and reflection should teach us that being a child of God is a dignity beyond any earthly accomplishment. If our sense of self-worth is firmly rooted in the conviction that we are important to God, we are far less likely to go astray in a frantic and disordered chase after human approval. We can enjoy competition and success without letting them dominate our lives. Just as important, we are far more likely to view other human beings as God wills.

Since God values ordinary people, we ought not judge them as inferior. Because we are children of God, we should see competition as a way of bringing out the best in ourselves and others, not as an opportunity to trample others under foot. Sport is far more enjoyable when athletes respect one another, when winners are humble in victory and losers are gracious in defeat.

Having considered God's attitudes toward humanity, we can refine our own attitudes by reflecting on the five limitations of Happiness Two. In the heat of competition, in the stress of academics, in the pressure of business, we can quickly forget that only one can win a race, that the elation of winning will pass, that we must not become hostages to the opinion of others, that other things are more important, and that our ability to win is eroded by time. We should consider these facts and pray about them until they become a foundational part of our value system.

OVERCOMING OBSTACLES

Of course, there are obstacles to be overcome, like advertising. Just as the media use bodily pleasure as a hook in advertising, so the media employ subtle and not-so-subtle ploys to deceive us into thinking that we will be admired for having this possession or that status symbol. We are more likely to be ridiculed than applauded if we drive a fancy car down the street in an effort to draw attention. Possessions may be useful, but they are not the measure of our worth. Francis of Assisi and Mother Teresa are among the most admired of human beings precisely because they valued people above things.

Another obstacle is an unreasonable striving for perfection. A talented professor once remarked, "When teaching a class, I can reach nineteen out of twenty students, but the one I don't reach can make me feel like I've failed." A speaker can hold ninety-five percent of the audience in rapt attention, but bored faces on the other five percent will cause a severe bout of depression. Why is this? On the one hand we may be troubled by insecurity. On the other we may expect too much of ourselves (not without a touch of vanity). One remedy for this misplaced guilt and damaged conceit is to reflect on the experiences of Jesus and Paul. When Jesus preached at the synagogue in his hometown, his listeners tried to kill him (Luke 4:29). Paul, on the other hand, killed one of his listeners with a lengthy sermon (Acts 20:9). Jesus and Paul didn't touch all those they addressed. Teachers, speakers, and parents should not expect to do so either.

A third obstacle is measuring ourselves against an imagined standard of perfection and selling ourselves short. We can have such an exaggerated fear of losing that we refuse to begin a project or enter a competition. Talented students may fail to get an advanced degree simply because they freeze at the idea of writing a thesis or taking an exam. High-school students may refuse to try out for a team because they dread failure. If we find ourselves afraid to participate in a worthwhile activity, we should pray for humility and courage. We've heard the old saying, "Anything worth doing is worth doing well." There's another old saying we should reflect on: "Anything worth doing is worth doing badly." We admire marathoners who run their race in spite of severe physical limitations. Their finish may be hours behind the winner, but it is a great accomplishment and a source of happiness to them, as well as an inspiration to others.

COMMANDMENTS AND VIRTUES

In striving for Happiness Two we should consider God's commandments, chiefly the seventh, eighth, and tenth. These commandments free us from damaging patterns of self-aggrandizement.

One reason people steal is to acquire material things and social status. This, of course, is forbidden by the seventh commandment. So is cheating at school, sports, games, business, or any other arena where breaking the rules might help us outstrip others. The eighth commandment proscribes lying, including the gossip that puts others down and the boasting that seeks to elevate ourselves. The tenth commandment prohibits the envy and jealousy which arise when we resent the achievements or success of another.

Then there are virtues to be cultivated, chiefly humility and a sense of humor. We dislike boasting and ostentation in others, and we should not tolerate them in ourselves. Humility disarms hostility, eradicates pettiness, and opens us up to the fun of competition. The great San Francisco 49ers quarterback, John Brodie, was once asked by a reporter why he accepted the ordinary task of holding the football for extra points and field goals. He grinned and replied, "Because if I don't, it will fall over." We can't help but smile at such humor and humility, qualities which make both sports and life more pleasant.

A sense of humor can help us accept both victory and defeat. I read about a little boy who kept telling his dad what a good hitter he was. So the dad said, "Let's see." They went out into the yard and the boy threw the ball up, swung, and missed. Two more tosses resulted in two more whiffs. "He looked at his dad and said, "I'm a good hitter, Dad, but I'm an even better pitcher."

Another virtue that can help us enjoy Happiness Two is gratitude, the antithesis of envy and jealousy. Modern advertising urges us to want more and better things. This means that we cannot enjoy what we have. Jerry told me that one day he sat on his twenty-five foot powerboat, not feeling as proud of it as usual because wealthy folks had docked their half-million dollar yacht next to him. Then he noticed that two fishermen had tied down their little bass boat nearby. They were admiring his craft. Looking more carefully at the people on the yacht, Jerry saw they were gazing with obvious envy at several children playing on a swing at the beach. Jerry saw in the episode a parable for today. "If we keep looking for what is bigger or better, we'll never be happy with what we have," he said. "And we'll eventually end up wishing for what we could have had all along." We must recognize the blessings we have and be grateful for them. Contentment is not having what we want, but enjoying what we have.

RAISING THE LEVEL OF COMPETITION

I've often been asked if praying is permissible at sports and other competitions. God is the giver of talent, and we may pray before competitions, asking God to help us do our best. Petitioning God to help us win is another issue. If God grants us victory, God must grant the other team defeat. If God wears any team's uniform, the competition is over. In a baseball game long ago, Joe Garagiola was at bat while his friend Yogi Berra caught for the other team. Joe drew a cross on the ground with his bat as a form of prayer. Yogi promptly erased it, smiled at Joe, and said, "How about if we just let God watch this game?"

But God is never merely a spectator. God keeps us in existence and is the source of life, strength, and fairness. So we should pray for God's blessings on the game at hand. We should pray that no one will be injured. We should ask God to let our competition result not in arrogant victory and in glorious defeat, but in mutual respect among winners and losers. Good sportsmanship and prayer can help us avoid Unhappiness Two and raise competition to the levels of Happiness Three and Four.

Happiness Two, like Happiness One, is enriched when it is deliberately integrated with higher levels of happiness. Coaches who promote team spirit among young athletes can foster friendships that last a lifetime. When teammates praise one another for success and encourage one another after mistakes, they elevate competition to the level of love. Families share affection at card games, and friendships are strengthened on tennis courts.

Happiness Two can flow into higher levels when we appreciate and applaud the accomplishments of others. Matthew loves sports. His grandparents attend his games and cheer every base hit and basket. There is no competition between them and their grandson. His achievements bring them joy. We too find happiness when we recognize the successes of others. We bring them happiness when we sincerely express our approval and admiration. Happiness Two expands into Happiness Three.

Business owners who are genuinely interested in their customers blend success and achievement with Christlike service. People who share their income with the needy turn earthly trophies into heavenly treasures (Matthew 6:19–21). John, a physician, retired early from his practice so that he could serve the poor in other countries. Over coffee one morning, he told me, almost apologetically, "I guess I could be driving a Lexus if I hadn't gone to Africa." No need to apologize. A car begins to depreciate the moment it is purchased. Service to the poor stores up wealth in heaven with interest that accrues forever. The achievement of Happiness Two blends into and is enriched with Happiness Three and Four.

And whatever we attempt or accomplish in sports, school, or work may be done for the glory of God. Athletes who pause before a game to say, "Thy will be done," and cooks who thank God for the food they prepare add a divine dimension to their efforts. What they do, by the grace of God, is "very good."

MOVING ON

It's a truism that no one ever said on a deathbed, "I wish I had devoted more time to my business." Death is nature's way of helping us see things as they really are, but then it's too late. Charles

Dickens' great classic, *A Christmas Carol*, is really a parable for all seasons, and it can teach us proper priorities now. Scrooge makes us realize that amassing wealth is more likely to win contempt than admiration and that putting possessions before people can chain us to burdens not easily cast off in this world or in the next. Like Scrooge, we take a huge step forward when we move on to Happiness Three.

REFLECTIONS

From card and board games to sporting contests, people love to compete. What are your favorite areas of competition? What have been your most notable experiences of Happiness Two? Of Unhappiness Two? The book lists five limitations of Happiness Two. Can you think of any others? Have you ever felt that you were being judged by the clothes you wore, by your possessions, or by other trappings related to Happiness Two? Have you ever judged others in this way? What are some examples of modern advertising that emphasize possessions or appearance as measures of our worth? Can you explain in your own words how God's esteem for you should be the foundation for your sense of self-worth? Who are people you've known who exemplify humility, humor, and gratitude? The book lists a number of ways Happiness Two can be integrated with higher levels of happiness. Can you name other ways?

THREE

HEART
Love Given and Love Lost

L ou and Corinne have been married for almost sixty years. Lou visits her daily at the nursing home where she has been confined with Parkinson's disease for five years. I met Lou there at noon one day and watched as he repeatedly gave her a tiny bit of food, then waited patiently as she struggled to swallow. After she was taken to her room, Lou and I went to a nearby restaurant. We talked about old times, then discussed Corinne's condition. Lou's eyes glistened with tears and his hands trembled. "I don't know what I'll do if Corinne dies first," he whispered. "I love her so much, and I can't imagine life without her."

The faithful love of husband and wife counts as one of the greatest blessings of human existence. Here there is no competition, no winning or losing, no ruler and ruled. Lou and Corinne are partners. They put each other first. The gift of self seems not a sacrifice but a grace. In sickness and in health, they find joy in caring for each other.

In so doing, they experience Happiness Three. Here the heart takes precedence, and they find contentment and satisfaction in loving, generous giving, and selfless service. So too can we. Happiness Three surpasses that of previous levels in duration, pervasiveness, and in the involvement of our human abilities. The joy that comes from true love can last for sixty years, and then some. It reaches to the very depths of our being and comes close to satisfying our deepest human longings for truth, beauty, and love. It moves beyond the satisfaction of bodily appetites and competitive urges to caring concern, thoughtful assessment of needs, deliberate choosing to do good for others, and generous sacrifice. It brings out the best in us as human beings.

Happiness Three may be found not just in married love, but in friendship and in any act of unselfish caring. It may be found in a life of service to others. Brandin is a young man of many talents, and could make a substantial income as a lawyer or stock broker. But he has chosen to be an elementary schoolteacher because he wants to help young children. Like him, teachers and nurses and social workers make monetary sacrifices to work in their fields, but they experience satisfaction in serving others.

Happiness Three results also from dedication to a worthy cause. It is felt by volunteers at hospitals and nursing homes, men and women who coach children's teams, Boy Scout and Girl Scout leaders, blood donors, and those who contribute to charitable works. People who step forward at times of crisis like the terrorist attacks of September 11, 2001, feel repaid by the very fact that they were able to help. Unselfish giving is indeed its own reward.

But Happiness Three does have limits. Lou and Corinne experience these limits as sixty years go by far too quickly. The greater their affection for each other, the more painful the prospect of parting. Teachers, nurses, and social workers find satisfaction in their vocations, but they also endure frustration and failure. And no matter how worthy a good cause may be, we eventually learn that it will not make this world perfect.

If we want to savor the best of Happiness Three without becoming disillusioned by its limitations, we must reflect and pray. Scripture can help us appreciate the joys of Happiness Three and accept its limits.

SCRIPTURE AND HAPPINESS THREE

Perhaps the most charming expression of generous love in the Old Testament is found in the Book of Ruth. A Jewish woman, Naomi, migrated with her husband and two sons from Bethlehem to Moab. There her sons married Moabite women, Orpah and Ruth. Then Naomi's husband and both her sons died. She decided to return to Bethlehem, and told her daughters-in-law to go back to their own families. Ruth refused to abandon Naomi, responding with some of the most beautiful words in Scripture: "Do not press me to leave you / or to turn back from following you! / Where you go, I will go; / Where you lodge, I will lodge; / your people shall be my people, / and your God my God. / Where you die, I will die— / there will I be buried" (Ruth 1:16–17). Ruth's devotion brought joy to Naomi, to Boaz, soon to became her husband, and to Ruth herself. She has been a model of love, commitment, and Happiness Three for countless generations since.

Scripture praises friendship as a prize of great value: "Faithful friends are a sturdy shelter: / whoever finds one has found a treasure. / Faithful friends are beyond price; / no amount can balance their worth" (Sirach 6:14–15). Friendship ranks above other sources of happiness: "Wine and music gladden the heart, / but the love of friends is better than either" (Sirach 40:20).

The Old Testament counsels concern for the poor and dedication to justice and peace, advising that these virtues bring happiness. "Happy are those who consider the poor; / the LORD delivers them in the day of trouble" (Psalm 41:1). "Thus says the LORD: / Maintain justice, and do what is right.... / Happy is the mortal who does this, / the one who holds it fast" (Isaiah 56:1–2).

The New Testament presents the greatest example of generous love in Jesus Christ. He is proof also of the gladness love can bring. Jesus said there can be no greater love than to give one's life for others. Christ's death on the cross brought him the joy of the Resurrection, and turned the pain of his disciples into joy (John 16:22).

Inspired by the life and teachings of Jesus, the first Christians experienced happiness in caring for one another and in sharing their belongings (Acts 2:44–47). The apostles, who had fled when Christ was arrested, found joy after his Resurrection even in persecution. When they were flogged at the command of Jewish authorities, "they rejoiced that they were considered worthy to suffer dishonor for the sake of the name" (Acts 5:41). In the Beatitudes, Jesus had promised happiness to those who would hunger and thirst for righteousness and work for peace. In the early Church we see that promise fulfilled.

SCRIPTURE AND UNHAPPINESS THREE

Happiness Three, however, can be terribly fragile in this imperfect world. On a beautiful spring day, Jim and Amy registered at our parish in Denver, Colorado. Jim was a commercial pilot who had married Amy after finishing a tour of duty as a Navy flyer. I remember being very impressed by their love for each other and their prospects for a wonderful life together. But less than a month later I received tragic news. Jim was piloting a private plane, with Amy and two friends as passengers. The plane's engine malfunctioned, and even Jim's skill and experience could not prevent a crash. He was killed. Amy was paralyzed from the waist down. I visited her in the hospital and we talked a long time. She spoke of Jim's love for her, how it had brought her so much happiness and drawn her into a closer relationship with God. "What did I do to deserve his love?" she asked. "And now, what will I do without him?"

Scripture reveals this fragility inherent in Happiness Three. The Book of Ruth does not hide the grief of Naomi as she returned to Bethlehem after the deaths of her husband and two sons. "I went away full, / but the LORD has brought me back empty" (Ruth 1:21). Throughout the Old and New Testaments, there are the sounds of sadness. Rachel, the wife of the patriarch Jacob, weeps from the other side of death for her children lost in the exile of Babylon (Jeremiah 31:15) and massacred by King Herod in his insane efforts to kill the baby Jesus (Matthew 2:18).

Scripture acknowledges that friendship can disappoint. "For there are friends who are such when it suits them, / but they will not stand by you in time of trouble" (Sirach 6:8). The closer the friendship the more dramatic its failure, as when Jesus was betrayed by Judas.

Helping others could bring joy to saints like Paul. It could also produce frustration and failure. Paul became exasperated at the sins of the Corinthians in their stumbling efforts to follow Christ as he rebuked them for partisanship, immorality, irreverence, and a host of other disorders. The Galatians drove him to distraction. "You foolish Galatians! Who has bewitched you? (...) I am afraid that my work for you may have been wasted" (Galatians 3:1; 4:11).

Likewise, those who dedicated their lives to the great cause of peace and justice eventually discovered that their dreams for a perfect world would not be realized this side of heaven. Isaiah foretold a world where the leopard would lie down to rest with the lamb. His vision of peace will be realized in eternity, not here. Someone has observed: "The leopard will lie down with the lamb, but the leopard will sleep a lot better!" Jeremiah became so frustrated with his failed efforts to lead people to peace and justice that he tried to hand in his resignation, which God refused to accept. "O LORD, you have enticed me, / and I was enticed; / you have overpowered me, / and you have prevailed. / I have become a laughingstock all day long; / everyone mocks me.... / If I say, 'I will not mention him, / or speak any more in his name,' / then within me there is something like a burning fire / shut up in my bones; / I am weary with holding it in, / and I cannot" (Jeremiah 20:7, 9).

Like Naomi, Rachel, Paul, and Jeremiah, we can be disappointed and frustrated in our efforts to love and help others, and in our eagerness to work for a good cause. How can we enjoy the best of Happiness Three without expecting more than human love and generous service can offer?

Our direction here will be different from that taken in the two lower levels. Whereas Happiness One and Two can drag us down with addictions and self-aggrandizement, Happiness Three tends to raise us up to the finest things in life. Whereas original sin inclines us to expect far more than Happiness One or Two can deliver, it disposes us to shy away from the effort required for love and service. Whereas modern advertising uses the immediate gratification of bodily appetites and the craving for recognition to coax us into buying things, it avoids transcendent values like love and sacrifice, whose rewards may be long in coming. To optimize Happiness Three, we must learn to appreciate its greatness, discipline ourselves to make the sacrifices necessary for effective works of charity and service, and realize that gratification from Happiness Three is often delayed. What is most important of all, we must understand that Happiness Three cannot be achieved if we make it our primary goal. Paradoxically, we find Happiness Three when we are concerned, not with our own happiness, but with that of others.

OPTIMIZING HAPPINESS THREE

Molly was an outstanding student, head cheerleader, and number one tennis player at her high school. Her family was well-to-do and Molly had everything she needed. But she was unhappy. She would often express her sadness by sitting in a rocking chair at home, rocking back and forth, refusing to talk to anyone. As Molly recalled this time in her life she said, "I think I took morbid satisfaction in the fact that my parents were really worried about me, but that didn't take away my misery." Then one of the teachers at school started a project which paired volunteer students with elderly people in the community. Molly decided to "adopt" an elderly woman who had no family. She noticed that visiting this lady, taking her to the grocery store, and running errands for her seemed to drive away the clouds of depression that darkened so much of her life. One day Molly, in a particularly bad mood, was rocking back and forth at home while family members tiptoed around her. Then she thought to herself, "This is crazy! Rocking back and forth just makes me more miserable. I'm going to see my old lady." She did, and from that day on she replaced the rocking chair with charity. Acts of love and service helped Molly enjoy life.

While getting a haircut from Al at the Golden Razor in Denver, Colorado, many years ago, I overheard Sandi, one of the other barbers, say, "I'm getting so excited about Christmas." This seemed rather unusual for a woman in her twenties, so I asked her why. "I think of all the people I'll be getting presents for," she replied, "and how happy it will make them when they open their gifts." Generosity brings more joy to those who give than to those who receive.

We should spend time thinking about such incidents, and about the really happy people we know. They are people who love generously, give freely without expecting rewards, and devote their lives to causes greater than themselves. Mother Teresa may be the most famous example of this, but every town has folks who radiate happiness because they find more joy in giving than in receiving. For Molly, for Sandi, for Mother Teresa, and for anyone who loves, Happiness Three takes us far beyond any satisfaction available from pleasure or competition.

Sacrifices are necessary if we wish to enjoy Happiness Three. Parents work long hours, give up much needed sleep, put up with temper tantrums, learn to discipline and to console, and at times wonder if children are worth the trouble. But then come the hugs, drawings to be placed on the fridge, piano recitals, hand-drawn cards on Mother's Day and Father's Day, and the many other compensations for "front-line-duty" that make parents say they wouldn't swap places with anyone. Swinging singles may seem to have a more enjoyable life, but considerable research has shown that parents have a much higher level of happiness, and swinging singles have a much higher suicide rate. Sacrifice is never easy, but sacrificial love brings joy.

When I was a younger priest and stationed in a busy parish with an older pastor and associate (both of whom had hearing aids), I was the one who answered the phone at night. On many occasions, I would be summoned to the local hospital after midnight, feeling sorry for myself that no one else could hear the phone. Invariably, I would return to the rectory grateful for the opportunity to minister to a person in need. Since then I've come to admire doctors on call who might get several phone calls at night, but respond cheerfully and without complaint. They know instinctively what it took me a long time to learn. Loving sacrifice produces happiness. It is a lesson we should all master and practice.

A delicious meal brings immediate delight. Not so every act of love. A mother must carry a baby within her womb for nine months while enduring morning sickness, a sore back, and ill-fitting clothes. Only then comes the reward of holding her baby in her arms. Parents must change countless diapers and clean up messes beyond measure before a child is old enough to say "Thank you." Teachers and medical personnel spend many years in preparation before they feel the satisfaction of helping others. Accepting the fact that gratification may be delayed is part of the discipline of making Happiness Three a component of our life plan.

But we should also enjoy the fact that love's recompense can sometimes be as swift as it is delightful. An unexpected hug from a little child. A smile from a friend we've helped. The contentment and peace we feel on the way home from serving food at a homeless shelter.

Finally, there is an elusiveness to Happiness Three that must be addressed. Happiness Three can be the result of genuine love. It can never be the motive. Parents who want to have children because they expect those children to make them happy will likely cause misery for children and themselves. Professors who walk into a classroom looking for admiration and praise will not teach well. A friendship sought because the other is influential, entertaining, or useful is not friendship, but self-seeking. If I seek my own good rather than that of others, I have regressed to Happiness Two, and will not experience the joy of Happiness Three. There is more happiness in giving than in receiving, but we must never confuse the one with the other.

HAPPINESS THREE AND FAMILY LIFE

God made Adam and Eve for each other, bade them to increase and multiply, and in so doing, established the family. There is no human institution more important for our happiness. People can endure poverty and obscurity and still be happy if their family life is strong. But no amount of money or fame will bring contentment if one's family is in turmoil. Whether we are married, widowed, separated, divorced, or single, we have family ties. We must take these into account if we wish to enjoy Happiness Three.

Of all the elements necessary for family happiness, none is more significant than the realization that love is primarily a decision, not a feeling. Love is the decision to do what is best for the other, no matter how we feel. Decisions are matters of the will and are made at our command. Feelings come and go. They are not entirely under our control. A life ruled by feelings is a rudderless ship tossed on a stormy sea. Genuine love is the sturdy rudder that guides us to the port of happiness we seek for ourselves and for our family.

True love, and the decisions that flow from love, guide us through the stages that are part of relationships between spouses, friends, parents and children. First, there is the stage of fresh affection, when all seems easy and light. Newlyweds see each other as perfect. Parents bring their new baby home. A third-grade girl thinks her dad is the greatest man on earth. Then comes a period of disillusionment. Faults appear. The baby cries all night. The little girl grows into a difficult teenager. This can lead to a third stage of real misery. Husbands and wives quarrel. Parents are tempted to harm a helpless child. A teen refuses to speak for days. If real love is present, a fourth stage will evolve as people come to accept and care for one another. Each one realizes: "Since I am not perfect, I cannot expect others to be perfect. As I want to be loved, so must I love others." This acceptance leads to the fifth stage, Happiness Three, the result of caring, forgiving, generous love.

I once read about a conversation between a young couple and another that had enjoyed a long, happy marriage. The younger husband asked the older what he had done to help make the relationship successful. He said, "When my wife does something that upsets me, I go into the bathroom. I close the door behind me. I walk over to the mirror, look in, and say, 'You're no bargain either!'" That's down-to-earth advice that can help anyone learn to accept and love others, and so bring happiness to self and family.

When problems come, as they surely will, we need patience. We may need to seek professional help. Gail told me about a friend of hers whose husband said he wanted a divorce. The woman took their children out of school, put the house up for sale, filed for divorce, and moved out of state—all within nine days. Her anger and her desire to "get it over with" might have been understandable, but she was gravely mistaken. Couples who seek help and work on their problems have to make sacrifices, but the long-term benefits make the sacrifices worthwhile. A couple I admired very much admitted they had struggled for the first twenty-five years of their marriage, but had finally arrived at a degree of happiness they would not exchange for anything in the world.

MOVING EVER UPWARD

Happiness Three can be enhanced when people look to God to purify and strengthen their ability to love and serve. Couples who obey God's commandments will be faithful and committed. "You shall not commit adultery" proscribes a sin that is much praised in the media, but destructive to love and happiness. "You shall not covet your neighbor's wife" points out the danger that lies within lustful thoughts and desires. "Honor your father and mother" counsels loving relationships between parents and children of every age. God's commandments shield us from Unhappiness Three and guide us to Happiness Three.

Jesus teaches that the greatest commandment is to love God and the second to love one's neighbor. The New Testament assures us that love of God and love of neighbor are closely interrelated. "Beloved, since God loved us so much, we also ought to love one another. No one has ever seen God; if we love one another, God lives in us, and his love is perfected in us" (1 John 4:11–12). We can therefore expect that loving other human beings will lead us closer to the love of God. We can also expect that God will help us to love one another. Research shows that couples who pray and worship together have a higher rate of success in marriage than those who do not.

We learn from Jesus that our concept of family should not be limited to those who happen to be with us on earth now. When Jesus was making his way to Jerusalem for the final time, he warned his apostles about the suffering and death he was soon to endure. They could not fathom his meaning. But heavenly visitors could and did. On the Mount of Transfiguration, Moses and Elijah came to Jesus. "They appeared in glory and were speaking of his departure, which he was about to accomplish at Jerusalem" (Luke 9:31). When Jesus endured such agony in the Garden of Gethsemane that he sweated blood, "an angel from heaven appeared to him and gave him strength" (Luke 22:43).

Angels watch over us and guard us (Matthew 18:10). Saints, like Moses and Elijah, who have gone before us are witnesses of the race we run (Hebrews 12:1). By the power of Christ's Resurrection, those who have died can touch us and strengthen our faith (Matthew 27:52–53). If Jesus received comfort and strength from saints and angels, we can expect comfort and strength in their company and under their protection.

Cheryl was critically injured in an automobile accident. She felt her spirit leaving her body, but before losing consciousness she whispered a prayer. Instantly, fear was replaced by peace. She experienced the nearness and love of her grandparents, who had been dead for some time. Their presence seemed mysterious, but very real, and she calmly accepted death or life as God willed. She awoke in a hospital, sure that she had been in the presence of saints who had gently ushered her back from their world to this one.

Cheryl learned from her experience that the doorway of death is a portal to peace, life, and love. The love of her grandparents opened her heart to the love of God. Death may seem to put an end to Happiness Three. It certainly demonstrates that earthly happiness cannot satisfy our deepest longings. But those longings, strengthened by God's promises and by angels and saints, lead us to a happiness that will fill us to the brim.

Lou dreads the very thought of life without Corinne. The prospect of separation brings tears to his eyes. But Lou is a man of faith. And so he is not without hope. He knows that any parting will be temporary. He and Corinne will be together again. Their mutual love, their faith, their hope, lead them to Happiness Four. We too seek this joy. We find it in God alone.

REFLECTIONS

Do you know couples like Lou and Corinne whose love and commitment are an inspiration to you? The book states that Happiness Three "comes close to satisfying our deepest longings for truth, beauty, and love." Do you agree? Why does Happiness Three only "come close" to satisfying these longings? In addition to the Book of Ruth, what other Bible stories of friendship and generous love can you recall? Which is your favorite? Have you ever had high hopes for a good cause, only to have that cause fall short of your expectations? What caused the failure? Have you studied the research showing that swinging singles are actually less happy than married couples? Does this fact surprise you? Why or why not? "Love is primarily a decision." This statement implies that more than a decision is involved. What else does love include? This chapter lists several Bible passages showing an interrelationship between those in heaven and us on earth. Can you think of any other passages? Have you heard of experiences like Cheryl's, of the interaction between heaven and earth described in Scripture?

FOUR

SOUL
God Fills Our Every Longing

℘

Bodily pleasure, worldly success, human love, all leave us restless and unsatisfied. Nothing on earth can fulfill our longings for perfect happiness, love, truth, beauty, and goodness. These longings are evidence that we are made for something more. For Someone more.

Clifford sought happiness in all the wrong places. Just out of high school he turned to crime and the highs of alcohol and drugs. Arrested for two murders committed to obtain drug money, he was convicted and sentenced to death. During his twelve years on death row he came to know Jesus through the ministrations of a kindly chaplain and was baptized. He apologized to the families of the men he had murdered, took full responsibility for what he had done, and professed his readiness to accept death. On the night before his execution, Clifford attended a Mass celebrated by the chaplain for him and several of his friends on death row. One of them wrote that Clifford wanted me to know how much he had enjoyed our home-study program, but that from now on he would go "straight to the Source of all Truth." On the day of his execution he said to his friends: "I love you. I'm glad you were part of my life. Remember, today I will be with my Jesus in paradise." His last words were, "Father, into your hands I commend my spirit." Clifford found at last the happiness for which he had been born.

Our hearts are restless until they rest in God. There is no need to search elsewhere for lasting joy. The yearnings of our hearts are themselves a sign that Someone exists to satisfy them. Eyes are evidence of objects to be seen. Ears suggest there are sounds to be heard. Our hearts' longings portend a God who is limitless love, truth, beauty, and goodness.

And it is our great good fortune to live at a time when incredible discoveries in astronomy, physics, microbiology, and other sciences testify to God's presence and power in ways previous generations could never have imagined. They give us assurance that God exists and that in God we will find the happiness we desire.

THE HEAVENS TELL GOD'S GLORY

"The heavens are telling the glory of God; / and the firmament proclaims his handiwork" (Psalm 19:1). The psalmist was in awe of the heavens, the sun and moon and planets and stars. We know much more about the heavens than the psalmist did, for we have the Hubble telescope, space travel, computers, and a host of other technological marvels that open our eyes to the wonder of creation.

If the psalmist had been asked to count the stars, he might have guessed at thousands, or perhaps millions. How many stars exist in our Milky Way galaxy, in our universe?

Astronomers report that there are at least one hundred billion stars in our own galaxy. They estimate the number of galaxies in the universe at over one hundred billion, each on the average with a hundred billion stars. These numbers are impossible to imagine. Mathematicians state that if we tried to count to one hundred billion, without stopping to eat or sleep, we would need eight hundred years. (When speaking to teachers or parents, I suggest they tell unruly children: "Go to the corner and count to one hundred billion, and don't come back until you are finished!")

As astonishing as the numbers are the distances in space, so vast that scientists must use light-years to measure them. In one second, light travels 186,282 miles, about seven times around the equator. In a year, light travels approximately six trillion miles. Alpha Centauri, the star closest to our sun, is about four and a half light-years away. To get there in our fastest spaceship would require eighty thousand years. Even if we could travel at the speed of light, we'd never visit much of God's creation. Going from one end of the known universe to the other at light speed would take thirty billion years.

The heavens are definitely telling the glory of God, and scientists are listening. The cover article of *Newsweek* magazine, July 20, 1998, was titled, "Science Finds God." It related that some of the most brilliant astronomers of our time, like Dr. Allan Sandage, have moved from atheism to belief because of the magnificence and complexity of the universe. The question, "Why is there something rather than nothing?" eludes science. The material universe, which had a beginning and is moving toward an end, cannot have caused itself. Either it came from nothing, or it was created by an all-wise, all-powerful Being who exists outside the limits of space and time. Albert Einstein showed that matter in all its forms is condensed energy. His famous equation, $E = mc^2$, meaning that energy equals matter times the speed of light squared, shows that energy and matter are interchangeable. Therefore, it makes sense to say that God, who is infinite energy and wisdom, could create a material universe. It makes no sense to say that all the matter in the universe could have come from nothing.

This should reassure us, who may sometimes wonder if our longing for God is just a cruel hoax. The hard evidence points to the reality of Someone who can fill our emptiness. Infinite love, goodness, truth, and beauty are found in God, and we can dare to be joyful because a universe thirty billion light-years across tells the glory of God.

GOD IN THE DETAILS

God is found not only in the vastness of the universe, but in the intricacy of its details. Dip your finger into a glass of water. Let one drop roll from your fingertip. Water seems ordinary and simple. But just as scientists have found boundless expanse in the universe, so they have discovered astounding complexity in its smallest components. Catch another drop of water on your fingertip. Let it fall to the ground. How many atoms do you suppose are in that single drop?

Atoms are so small that they cannot be seen, but they can be measured. How many exist in a drop of water? Imagine all six billion people on earth counting these atoms at the rate of one per second, so that we are counting six billion atoms per second. To number the atoms at this rate, we'd need twenty thousand years.

The nature and behavior of atoms and the subatomic particles of which they are composed are the subject matter of quantum physics. The facts scientists have discovered in this field are so astonishing that no one claims to understand them completely. One hundred years ago, some physicists foolishly thought they knew everything about the makeup of the universe. In their closed system there was no possibility of miracles, no room for God. Now some scientists are saying that in the realm of quantum physics, miracles are not only possible, they are to be expected. Behind those miracles is the same God who created the universe.

Perhaps the most amazing discoveries in the small, small world have been those in the field of microbiology. How many atoms are there in an average adult human body? The answer is 10^{28}, or 1 followed by twenty-eight zeros, more atoms than there are stars in the universe (of which there are at least one hundred billion times one hundred billion).

In our bodies, atoms are the building blocks of molecules which in turn are the building blocks of human cells. Each cell is a fabulously complex mini-factory interacting with other cells to produce the structure for growth, activity, thought, emotions, and the many other elements of human life. An average adult body contains about seventy-five trillion cells. Every second, each of these seventy-five trillion cells produces approximately two thousand proteins from combinations of three hundred to one thousand amino acids.

When I'm speaking to couples, I suggest to the men: "Next time you are watching a football game and your wife complains that you are doing nothing, tell her, 'Honey, what do you mean I'm doing nothing? In just the last second my body produced seventy-five trillion times two thousand proteins from combinations of three hundred to one thousand amino acids.'" After I mentioned this at a diocesan religious education conference, one wife rolled her eyes and said ruefully, "Now I'll never get him away from the TV."

We may be composed of seventy-five trillion cells, but we were once just a single cell smaller than the head of a pin. In that cell were all the directions for who we are today: our size, the color of our eyes, whether we are right-handed or left-handed, everything. Scientists assert that if we printed out these directions, we would need two hundred books the size of the New York City telephone directory. Many scientists (including former atheists) maintain that this marvelous order and complexity cannot be an accident. Where there is such magnificent design, there must be a Designer.

Some theorists used to claim that life was just the chance combination of elements that began to bump into one another billions of years ago and eventually transformed themselves into the components necessary for life. Scientists now say that the complexity of living cells is so extreme that they could not have been formed accidentally even in the fifteen billion years the universe has been in existence.

To get a sense of the difficulty in producing by chance the human cell that was our beginning, imagine a huge box full of letters and numbers. Shake that box until you have a perfect edition of the New York City phone directory, each name spelled correctly, placed in alphabetical order, matched with its proper address and phone number. Do this with two hundred different boxes. How long would it take? Many scientists say that forever would not be long enough. If there is no God, cellular complexity and design must have come about in an accident far more unlikely. Given a phone directory, we presume intelligence, not chance, behind it. Given human life, we are wise to presume Intelligence behind it as well.

We look at the stars, at a drop of water, at our own bodies, and we see the handiwork of Someone who outstrips our abilities beyond imagining. God is out of our league! At times we may think of God as a kindly senior citizen who is just a bit more intelligent than we are, who works hard at arranging and operating the universe. No. God is omnipotent, all-powerful. God could turn the universe upside down with a mere thought. God is omniscient, all-knowing. God knows the number of atoms in the body of every human being, and God knows the number of atoms in the universe.

Every day seems to bring new discoveries revealing God's presence in our world. Recent experiments, for example, indicate that our brains are designed to contact God. In the sixteenth century, Saint John of the Cross wrote that we can have our most direct experience of God if we detach ourselves from sensory stimuli as much as possible. Brain scans now show that people deep in contemplation produce a distinct pattern of neural activity where information flowing from the senses slows dramatically and the mind experiences a sensation of transcendence and unity with God. What Saint John taught has a basis in biology. Our brains are wired for God in the same way they are wired for light. Seeing light stimulates a part of the brain designed to receive and analyze light. Contemplation stimulates a part of the brain designed to experience union with God.

If you'd like to delve into modern scientific findings and their relationship to religion, I'd recommend two excellent books: *More Than Meets The Eye*, by Richard A. Swenson, M.D. (Navpress), and *The Hidden Face of God*, by Gerald L. Schroeder (The Free Press), the sources for most of the scientific information given in this section.

Now we must get down to practicalities.

GOD AND US

Can this God, the maker of galaxies and atomic particles, make us happy? Spend a few moments reflecting on the scientific facts just outlined. The answer becomes obvious. It should bring a smile to the face of the gloomiest pessimist.

All the more when we realize that we hunger for love, and find happiness in being loved. God is not an impersonal power plant on the outer reaches of space. The New Testament reveals that "God is love" (1 John 4:16). God is a loving community of three Persons—Father, Son, and Holy Spirit. We cannot fully understand this Trinity of Persons in one divine nature, but we must realize that the Trinity has tremendous consequences for our own happiness. We are, after all, made in the image and likeness of God, and we can catch a glimpse of the Trinity by looking at ourselves.

We glance into a mirror and recognize our image. We know ourselves, and this idea, this mental picture, is real. We love ourselves, and this love is real. God the Father knows himself from all eternity, but God's knowledge is so infinitely perfect that it is a person, the Son. The Father and Son love each other with a love so infinitely perfect that it is a person, the Holy Spirit. From this eternal and unlimited knowledge and love flow the design and reality of the entire universe, expressed when God created all things, including us. Since we have been made by God, who is perfect knowledge and love, we hunger for perfect truth and love. That hunger will be satisfied only to the extent that we know and love, and are known and loved. This is what Augustine meant when he said, "You have made us for yourself, O Lord, and our hearts are restless until they rest in you."

As we shall see in the next chapter, our life on earth is transitional. We are placed in time so that we may be outfitted for eternity. We learn to know and love here so that we may know and love perfectly in heaven. "Beloved, we are God's children now; what we will be has not yet been revealed. What we do know is this: when he is revealed, we will be like him, for we will see him as he is" (1 John 3:2). "For now we see in a mirror, dimly, but then we will see face to face. Now I know only in part; then I will know fully, even as I have been fully known" (1 Corinthians 13:12–13).

This brings us back to the catechism answer explaining why we exist: "God made me to know, love, and serve him in this world, and to be happy forever." To the extent that our lives remain oriented toward God, to that extent will we be happy here and equip ourselves for eternal happiness. If we depart from the path that leads to God, we will be unhappy. So we can enjoy pleasure and success and human love when these fit into a pattern that leads to God. Outside that pattern, everything, no matter how attractive it may initially appear to be, will ultimately bring frustration and misery.

As we search for God, let it be with the awareness that God loves us to extremes as vast as the borders of the universe. We may have measured God's love by daring to hope that God might care for us as much as our best friend does. Not even close! God made from nothing a universe of one hundred billion galaxies. No human being can create even a single galaxy. We can conclude from this that God is at least one hundred billion times as great as any human being. God is love. Therefore, God loves each one of us at least a hundred billion times as much as any human being could love us.

This is Good News. But it gets better. "So we have known and believe the love that God has for us. God is love, and those who abide in love abide in God, and God abides in them" (1 John 4:16). Not only does God love us, but God is accessible. If we lived next door to a famous athlete or movie personality, friends would likely consider us fortunate. They might ask us to get an autograph for them. But God outshines the greatest celebrity as the sun outshines a firefly. There are no walls around God's estate. There are no bodyguards shielding God from our attention. We need not make an appointment. There are no waiting lines. The One who can make us truly happy abides in us.

SCRIPTURE AND HAPPINESS FOUR

Happiness Four in its perfection, eternal union with God, was revealed in Old Testament times. "The souls of the righteous are in the hands of God... / their hope is full of immortality.... / In the time of their visitation they will shine forth" (Wisdom 3:1, 4, 7). Jesus taught the reality of eternal life: "This is indeed the will of my Father, that all who see the Son and believe in him may have eternal life; and I will raise them up on the last day" (John 6:40).

But Scripture shows that Happiness Four is available to us here and now. The psalmist asks the question, "What can bring us happiness?" He answers the question at once: "Let the light of your face shine on us, O Lord" (Psalm 4:6, Grail Translation, Collins: London, 1963). Both the Old and New Testaments assure us that real happiness is to be found in God. The Jews did not have the Hubble telescope or electron microscopes, but they marveled at God's creation. In their poetic imagery, all things find happiness at being God's handiwork: "Let the heavens be glad, and let the earth rejoice; / let the sea roar, and all that fills it; / let the field exult, and everything in it. / Then shall all the trees of the forest sing for joy / before the LORD" (Psalm 96:11–13).

The psalmist found happiness in God's presence: "How lovely is your dwelling place, / O LORD of hosts!… / Happy are those whose strength is in you…. / O LORD of hosts, / happy is every-one who trusts in you" (Psalm 84:1, 5, 12). "You show me the path of life. / In your presence there is fullness of joy; / in your right hand are pleasures forevermore" (Psalm 16:11).

When Jesus Christ became one of us, his Mother's first re-sponse was happiness in God's presence: "My soul magnifies the Lord, and my spirit rejoices in God my Savior" (Luke 1:46–47). An angel announced that Christ's birth was "good news of great joy" (Luke 2:10). Many years later Jesus would assure his apostles that he had come to offer them friendship and union with God, to give them his joy and to make their joy complete (John 15:9–15). Incredibly, he does this for us by making his own joy com-plete in us (John 17:13).

Jesus explains the most powerful expression of this reality in his words to a large crowd of disciples at Capernaum: "I am the living bread that came down from heaven…. Those who eat my flesh and drink my blood have eternal life, and I will raise them up on the last day; for my flesh is true food and my blood is true drink. Those who eat my flesh and drink my blood abide in me, and I in them" (John 6:51, 55–56). These words were so startling that they caused many of his disciples to walk away. They simply couldn't believe what Jesus was telling them (John 6:61–66). The apostles did believe, and they were with Jesus at the Last Supper when he said over bread and wine, "This is my body…this is my blood" (Matthew 26:26, 28). As we try to grasp the meaning of these words, we must do so with the realization that Jesus is the God who created a universe of one hundred billion galaxies and who loved us so much that he died on the cross for our salvation.

For the Jews, the body was the person, and blood was life. So when Jesus said, "This is my body...my blood," he was saying in both cases, "This is myself." When explaining these words of Jesus to children, I ask them to recall pictures of themselves when they were infants. "Were you still the same person you are today?" "Yes," they answer. Next I invite them to imagine how big they will be in high school or college. "But you will still be the same person?" "Yes," they chorus back. "You see," I explain, "There is something that makes you who you are and it doesn't depend on size or shape. That's how it was with Jesus. There was something that made him who he was as a tiny infant in the manger and as an adult dying on the cross. But Jesus is God, and he can do something we can't. Jesus can take everything that makes him Jesus and fill the bread and wine with himself. The bread and wine then become Jesus. When you receive him, he then fills you with himself. Now your eyes are the eyes of Jesus. Your hands are the hands of Jesus. Remember his words, 'Those who eat my flesh and drink my blood abide in me, and I in them.' And why would he want to be so close to you that he lives in you? Well, you want to be close to those you love. You hug your parents and grandparents. So Jesus wants to be close to you, so close that he lives in you and you in him."

As we ponder Jesus' words in John 6 and Matthew 26, we must open our hearts to a God who loves us a hundred billion times as much as any human being could love us. He wants to be a hundred billion times closer to us than we can be to any human being. His words, "This is my body, my blood," should prepare us for the most magnificent share of Happiness Four available this side of heaven.

OTHER EXPRESSIONS OF HAPPINESS FOUR

Happiness in God, Happiness Four, may be experienced in many other ways. We find peace and contentment in discovering that life has meaning. We have the security of knowing how to live well. We learn that suffering and death can be overcome. We look forward to eternal union with God and with our loved ones in heaven. These assurances of faith do not depend on the vagaries of emotion or circumstance. They are God's Word. They are the solid rock upon which a happy life can be built.

Once we know God through his Son, Jesus Christ, we can learn to recognize Happiness Four at special moments in life. The elation of parents at the birth of a child. A moment's delight at worship as beautiful music touches our spirit. An awe-filled recognition of God's signature on a spectacular mountain vista. Great saints may have such moments of ecstasy more often than the rest of us, but we can learn to recognize God as the source of such happiness.

We should not expect unending bliss on this earth, but we can discover in the Bible, in prayer, and in good people that God is always present, always loving us, always ready to add a dimension of joy to everything we do.

We have sampled a few Bible passages that tell us to look to God for happiness. There are countless others. In private Scripture reading and at worship we should be attentive to them. In Chapter Seven we will discuss prayer and spirituality as avenues to Happiness Four. Let's look now at other ways to open ourselves to the happiness God wants us to have.

THE COMMANDMENTS AND
HAPPINESS FOUR

In Chapter One we saw that original sin overturned the priorities God had established. We are too easily attracted to the satisfaction of bodily appetites and to the trappings of success. Modern advertising recognizes this and uses the lure of pleasure and possessions to entice us into purchasing more and more. On the other hand we tend, like Adam and Eve after the Fall, to hide from God. We may give less attention to God than to the television. And television ads seldom use God to catch our interest. So if we want to find Happiness Four we will have to work at it.

A good place to begin is the Ten Commandments. Those relating to God are placed first, a gentle hint from the Author about their importance. "I am the Lord your God. You shall not have other gods beside me." In Moses' time people actually made idols and worshiped them. We are more likely to worship pleasure, possessions, power, and popularity. A quick review of Chapters One and Two should remind us that these things have their place. But when they are put on life's pedestal and begin to push God to the background, they bring unhappiness, not joy.

"You shall not take the name of the Lord your God in vain." We express our respect and love for others in the way we use their names. We do not greet a parent or close friend in the way we might address an aggressive dog trying to chase us from its territory. Jesus taught us to call God our Father. We are God's children, and if we want to find happiness in the relationship we will acknowledge it by a reverent use of God's name. We cannot use God's name in curses or in careless phrases without damaging our bond of love with the Lord.

"Remember to keep holy the Lord's day." In Genesis, God rests on the seventh day to establish a pattern of behavior for us.

The Jewish people set aside Saturday as a day of rest. Christians, to honor Christ's Resurrection, observe Sunday as the Lord's day (Acts 20:7). Old Testament prophets insisted on the importance of the Sabbath as a way to happiness: "Happy is the mortal who ...keeps the Sabbath" (Isaiah 56:2). New Testament Christians met regularly for the "breaking of bread" (Acts 2:42) to commemorate the Lord's Supper and the Lord's death and Resurrection. The importance of regular Sunday worship cannot be overemphasized. Today it is fashionable to disparage worship as mere religiosity, to proclaim that one can find God elsewhere just as well. But it is impossible to be a devoted follower of Christ if we disregard God's commandment and Christ's own request.

Jesus asked us to do many things for others and ourselves. There is only one thing he asked us to do for him: "This is my body, which is given for you. Do this in remembrance of me" (Luke 22:19). How can we claim to follow Jesus or find joy in him if we refuse this appeal?

God requests so little of us. On the average, if we live to be eighty years old, we will spend about three and a half years reading, five years talking, six years getting an education, six years riding in a car, seven years eating, eleven years watching television and recreating, fourteen years working, and twenty-seven years sleeping. If we live to be eighty and spend an hour worshiping God every Sunday and five minutes praying every day, it adds up to...six months. How can we refuse so little to a loving God who has given us so much?

If we are still unconvinced, we should review the many studies which show that regular Sunday worship is good for our physical, mental, and emotional health, all important for our happiness. God does know what is best for us.

The first three commandments direct us toward joyful union with God. A consideration of separation from God, Unhappiness Four, can also help us stay on the path to lasting joy.

UNHAPPINESS FOUR

If knowing God is Happiness Four, Unhappiness Four is the opposite, not knowing God. When human beings deliberately reject God by serious sin, by deliberate neglect, or by siding with Satan, they hide from God as surely as did Adam and Eve in the Garden. If one's deliberate rejection of God remains through death, Unhappiness Four is hell, eternal separation from God. Hell is the sum of the most awful experiences of this life carried through to eternity. The New Testament uses imagery like fire, wailing, and gnashing of teeth to describe the pain of hell. These are frightful terms, but they barely describe the worst pain of those in hell, knowing that the one thing that could have brought them happiness, God's love, is what they have set themselves against forever.

There is a hell on earth too. It is experienced in the despair of those who do not believe in God, who think that life has no meaning. It is lived by those who can find no value in suffering. It shadows those who suppose that pleasure or success will bring lasting joy. It haunts those who reject the commandments, who seek to harm others, who hold God in contempt.

Unhappiness Four is unimaginable misery. We need not spend a great deal of time considering it, but we should be aware of its reality. Jesus taught us to fear hell because a healthy fear of what is evil can impel us to seek what is good.

GOD'S TOUCH

Observance of the commandments will heighten our sensitivity to times when God seems to reach out and touch us gently, reassuring us that we are not alone. We need to recognize these occasions, remember them, and allow them to gladden our hearts.

THE SEARCH FOR HAPPINESS

We should discern God's gentle smile behind such loving touches. I will refer to three of these: "coincidences" that have the stamp of divine Providence because they are more than coincidences, children who see God where our weary eyes fail to discern the divine, friends who feel the hand of God when they are most in need.

"Coincidences"

While having dinner with friends one evening, I was paged by our answering service and asked to call a family in the parish. Due to emergency medical expenses, the family was in desperate need of three hundred dollars. I told the family I'd do what I could, then returned to dinner without saying anything to those around the table. After the meal, the couple who had invited me to their home said they wanted to express their gratitude to God for some recent blessings. They handed me a check for three hundred dollars. It might have been a coincidence, but all the way home I kept remembering the old saying, "A coincidence is just another name for a miracle when God wishes to remain anonymous."

Children

Jeff and Tina were expecting their third child with eager anticipation. But Tina miscarried after fourteen weeks. She had to remain in the hospital for a day, and Jeff gently told their two daughters, Katie, age three, and Makenda, age five, what had happened. Later that afternoon Makenda explained to us at an outdoor family gathering: "Mommy is very sad because the baby was born too early and died. The baby is a spirit and we can't see the baby." Then, she pointed to a bird flying high above, and added, "But the baby went to heaven, just like that bird up there." Through Makenda, God touched us. God's wisdom does come from the mouths of babes.

Friends Who Feel the Hand of God

Leo and Linda and their three children were driving from their home in Florida to visit Leo's family in Iowa. Their van broke down on an isolated country road about thirty miles from Cedar Falls. Leo looked under the hood and couldn't find the problem. One of their children became upset at their situation and began to cry. Linda tried to calm her and said a prayer with the children. As they prayed, a huge monarch butterfly settled on Leo's shoulder, then fluttered over to the upraised hood. Linda pointed it out to the children, saying that perhaps this was God's way of letting them know everything would be okay. Then, amazingly, in that isolated place, a tow truck appeared. The driver stopped and asked if he could help. Leo gratefully accepted his offer, then inquired why he happened to be on that road. The man said he didn't really know. He had come from Illinois to Cedar Falls to pick up a car, and chose this route, which he'd never driven before, on a lark. As the man hitched the van to his tow truck, the butterfly soared off into the sky. When they arrived at a garage in Cedar Falls, the driver refused payment. A man at the garage worked overtime to fix the van, and charged only expenses. As the family drove away, their son said to Leo and Linda, "I feel like we've been in an episode of *Touched by an Angel.*"

Coincidences that seem divinely planned, children who see God where we don't, friends who find God in unlikely places—these are ways God touches us. We should be attentive to them. We can't be guaranteed butterflies and tow trucks every time we pray in a troubling situation, but we will experience God's presence. And we can choose to accept the happiness that comes from being held in the palm of God's hand.

GRACE

Happiness Four comes also when we are aware of God's grace, Scripture's term for God's presence and power. "God's grace and mercy are with his elect" (Wisdom 4:15). We are "saved through the grace of the Lord Jesus" (Acts 15:11). Grace is God's life and love shared with us, the life and love rejected by Adam and Eve.

Life and love are rather abstract terms. To explain how God's grace can bring us happiness, I ask parents and grandparents if they've ever been given drawings by children. "Of course," they reply. I ask where they put the drawings, and the answer is invariably, "On the fridge." "Could these drawings be sold for a million dollars at an art auction?" "Of course not." "But how much are they worth to you? "They're priceless."

Notice how the love of a parent or grandparent imparts tremendous value to a picture drawn by a little child. That's what grace does. God's love imparts immeasurable worth to everything we do. God misses nothing. God puts even our tears in a bottle and keeps a record of them (Psalm 56:8). The fact that no good deed of ours is ever forgotten by God should be a source of lasting happiness.

While speaking to small children at a school in Little Rock, Arkansas, one morning. I explained that when they help others, their good deeds are posted by God on the fridge in heaven. One little girl said, "God must have an awfully big fridge." As a matter of fact, God does. It's thirty billion light-years across!

DEATH AND RESURRECTION
—THE WAY TO HAPPINESS

Seeing life's artwork on God's "fridge" is our ultimate goal. But this goal can be achieved only through suffering and death. God is love. God is good. God is life. Why, then, does God allow hatred? Why is there evil? Why must life on earth end in death?

There are no easy answers. But God lived the questions by becoming one of us. In Jesus Christ, in his death and Resurrection, we live the answers.

REFLECTIONS

Which of the facts related in the sections, "The Heavens Tell God's Glory" and "God in the Details," strike you as the most remarkable? Do such facts help you to believe in God's existence? What do you think of the statement that God loves each one of us at least a hundred billion times as much as any human being could love us? Read again the explanation of Jesus' words, "This is my body" found in the section, "Scripture and Happiness Four." How would you explain these words to a small child? Can you name some personal experiences, like a spectacular mountain vista or the birth of a child, that have caused you to feel the presence of God? How would you answer the question, "Why do we have to go to church?" The section, "God's Touch," lists three examples of God's reaching out to us. Have you had similar experiences? Have you heard about similar experiences? Can you explain grace in your own words?

FIVE

HAPPINESS, SUFFERING, AND DEATH

M ary was at her nurse's station in a small hospital. Her husband, who had been experiencing serious heart problems, was an administrator at the same hospital, and he was talking to another nurse in a waiting area. Suddenly Mary heard the other nurse say, "Joe, are you all right?" She looked up and saw her husband slowly collapse to the floor. She immediately began a code blue, trying to breathe life back into him. But as she did, he took one last breath, and she knew there would be no more. At once she felt a great sense of peace, realizing that the man she loved so much had sent his last breath into her lungs. Then she had an experience which she later described as otherworldly, but real: "I saw the Mother of Jesus take my husband by the hand and lead him to her Son." She retains an absolute conviction that her husband is enjoying new life with God, and this conviction has helped her find happiness and peace.

I have heard many such stories, encounters with angels and residents of heaven showing that life is not limited to this world. Jesus was consoled by Moses, Elijah, and an angel. Countless people with sound minds and healthy emotions have reported being touched by Jesus, by angels, and by saints. Dr. Diane Komp, a specialist in pediatric oncology at Yale University, records a number of such experiences in her beautiful book, *Images of Grace*. Dr. Komp was so convinced of the reality of these happenings that she moved from atheism to a firm belief in God and in Jesus as the Lord who leads us to eternal life. For her, dying children were a "window to heaven" through which she glimpsed the face of God. These children were ravaged by cancer but filled with peace and happiness. She herself found God and the peace of Happiness Four in a most unlikely place, a hospital ward for terminally ill children.

This should not surprise us. Christians find God on a most unlikely place, a hill of execution. On Calvary we see Jesus offer himself in history's greatest act of love, and we realize the incredible fact that God suffers with us. Standing at the foot of the cross with Jesus' own Mother, we begin to realize that the greatest obstacles to happiness, suffering and death, can be overcome.

WHY SUFFERING AND DEATH?

Why must there be suffering and death? How can I make sense of suffering and death? The answers to these questions are not easy, but they are linked to human freedom. God is love, and God created us to enjoy the great happiness that comes from loving and being loved. This requires freedom because love cannot be forced. If we are free to love, we must also be free to refuse love. Like Adam and Eve, we can say "no" to God as well as "yes." We can misuse the gift of freedom by disobeying God. In so doing, as we have seen in previous explanations of unhappiness at every level, we hurt ourselves and others. God allows this because otherwise we could not be free.

Perhaps we can see how God must allow people to hurt others if freedom is to be real. But what about evils that seem to come from nature, like cancer? In the last chapter we observed how scientists are learning about the vastness and incredible complexity of creation. God formed a universe of one hundred billion galaxies. He paid so much attention to detail that the atoms in a human body outnumber the stars in the universe. If God has such power and can design our bodies so magnificently, why must there be sickness, pain, and death?

Again, the answer is freedom. God gave wonderful abilities so we could cooperate with God in bringing this world to perfection. We might suppose that the world would be better if it were already perfect, but God knows that while we live in time we need to make a contribution. A world existing in time must be a world in process. Time allows the pleasures of the body, the possibility of competition, the satisfaction of achievement, the happiness of helping others in an imperfect world. Given the reality of time and the need we have to use our talents, we can see how God's plan for us is better than anything we might devise.

But down through the ages, people have used their talents for evil purposes as well as for good. Some individuals have campaigned against God's commandments and God's providential plan for humanity. As a result, awful wars and terrible evils have devastated our world. Immense possibilities for good have been left untouched. Most of the tragedies that darken our days could long ago have been eliminated by humanity's humble acceptance of God's designation of good and evil. Every disease could have been conquered. Harmony with nature—including nature's energies of fire, wind, water, and motion—could have been achieved. Our world could have been a natural transition to the eternal happiness that is our ultimate destiny.

But through countless ages humanity has repeated the refusal of Adam and Eve to let God be God. So we live in a world far short of what it should be. Disease, tragedy, grief, and the uncertainties of death trouble us and erode our ability to find happiness. God could have remedied this situation by simply annihilating us. But for reasons we may never fully comprehend, God entered into our woe. Jesus took upon himself the suffering of humanity. He carried the cross to forever unite himself to our pain. He died on that cross and rose in order to lead us through death to eternal joy.

DEATH IS BIRTH

Jesus accepted the cross "so that through death he might...free those who all their lives were held in slavery by the fear of death" (Hebrews 2:14–15). Death has its fearsome aspects, but Jesus helps us conquer fear by showing that death is not just an end but a new birth. We spent nine months in our mother's womb. We outgrew this environment, which could no longer sustain us. We died to life in the womb, but death turned out to be birth. We moved from darkness into light, and gazed into the eyes of one who had been with us from the beginning. We found ourselves in a world where there were opportunities for growth, knowledge, love and happiness that far surpassed anything in the womb.

By his death and Resurrection, Jesus proves that death is really another birth. Our body will wear out because of age, illness, or accident, and we will die. But once again darkness will turn into light. We will find ourselves face to face with Jesus, fully alive in a new world with opportunities for growth, knowledge, love, and happiness that go beyond anything on earth.

Catherine was so eager for these treasures stored up in heaven that she faced old age with peaceful confidence. She took delight in giving away her jewelry and other possessions to members of her family. Better things awaited her. On her deathbed, she said to her granddaughter, "Don't cry, Lovie. I'm not afraid of dying. I'm excited."

The assurance of eternal life is a source of joy to those who believe. It is Happiness Four on earth. At death it will be transformed into perfect bliss. We will see God "face to face" (1 Corinthians 13:12). The limits we endure here will be stripped away. "See, the home of God is among mortals. / He will dwell with them as their God; / they will be his peoples, / and God himself will be with them; / he will wipe every tear from their eyes. / Death will be no more; / mourning and crying and pain will be no more, / for the first things have passed away" (Revelation 21:3–4).

Cindy, a young woman dying of brain cancer, said in a newspaper interview: "Heaven's really going to be a neat place to go after you're through with all of this." How true! God's presence, the enjoyment of perfect beauty, truth, and goodness, the company of angels and saints, unfailing security and peace, all this and more will finally satisfy our restless hearts. We will possess Happiness Four in its fullness.

SUFFERING, HAPPINESS, AND HOPE

The hope of eternal beatitude is our best reason to be happy here and now. Hope has given courage to heroes who sacrificed their lives for others, strength to those working for justice, serenity to those who suffer. Courage, strength, and serenity are elements of Happiness Four that enabled martyrs to brave the sword, fire, and wild beasts. With Saint Paul they could say: "I consider that the sufferings of this present time are not worth comparing with the glory about to be revealed to us" (Romans 8:18). Hope in eternal life even allowed Paul to laugh at death: "When this perishable body puts on imperishability, and this mortal body puts on immortality, then the saying that is written will be fulfilled: 'Death has been swallowed up in victory. Where, O death, is your victory? Where, O death, is your sting?'" (1 Corinthians 15:54–55).

Hope still brings courage, strength, serenity, and the ability to laugh at death. Doctor Joe was a caring physician whose skill as a surgeon was matched by his love for his family and his devotion to God. Diagnosed with cancer, he fought the disease with courage and good humor. After recovering from a particularly difficult crisis, he wrote to say he was back on the golf course

"I'm not playing well," he mused, "but at least I'm looking down at the grass!" As the disease took its toll, he said he was ready to meet the Lord and wondered why the call didn't come. "Saint Peter must have a long line up there," he laughed. At exactly the right time, Jesus came, gently. As his wife, Dee, and son, Joseph, were praying the Our Father, Joe looked into Dee's eyes, breathed his last, then gazed upon the eyes of Jesus.

Mary Beth was a lovely young lady who died of cancer at the age of fifteen. Her care and concern for others were the inspiration for a foundation, *Mary Beth's Angels Foundation*, to benefit underprivileged children. Mary Beth's faith in Jesus, her undying hope, and her brave decision to be joyful in the face of death found expression in her motto: "Life is short. Laugh hard!" Her life was short by human standards, but it brought God's love to many. A large congregation attended her funeral service celebrated at the Saint Louis Cathedral by Archbishop Justin Rigali and Bishop David Ricken, her cousin. I'm certain that Mary Beth is now in heaven with a new motto: "Life here is forever. Laugh really hard!"

MEANING IN SUFFERING

Scripture teaches us to live in hope and to endure affliction for the sake of eternal happiness. But the New Testament also shows that suffering has meaning and value here and now. Consideration of this meaning and value can help us discover a dimension of happiness made possible through the passion and death of Christ.

Suffering can bring union with God. Some people erroneously feel that pain separates them from God. John, a good and generous man who experienced one health problem after another, said, "All this sickness makes me feel tired. But the worst part is that I used to feel close to God, and don't anymore. Something is wrong with my spiritual life." No. In fact, John may be very close to

God. Jesus experienced a sense of desolation on the cross: "My God, my God, why have you forsaken me?" (Matthew 27:46). In these words, taken from Psalm 22:2, Jesus expressed the desolation of all human beings who feel abandoned by God in their pain. On the cross Jesus denied himself the consolation of divinity. He let his physical sufferings flow into his mind, soul, and emotions. He then committed himself and all humankind into God's care: "Father, into your hands I commend my spirit" (Luke 23:46). We may feel that we are far from God when we suffer, but feelings are not facts. The facts are found in Scripture, and Christ's agony on the cross assures us that suffering does not separate us from God. Saint Paul endured a great deal of suffering, but realized that it united him to Jesus: "I have been crucified with Christ; and it is no longer I who live, but it is Christ who lives in me" (Galatians 2:19–20).

Suffering can help us grow in holiness. Holiness is the union of our will with God's, not only when this is easy, but when it is very difficult. In the Garden of Gethsemane, Jesus prayed, "My Father, if it is possible, let this cup pass from me; yet not what I want but what you want" (Matthew 26:39). We achieve holiness in the joyful acceptance of suffering and the afflictions of old age. I once had the privilege of meeting Sister Frances, a nun in her late nineties who was confined to a wheelchair yet vibrant and cheerful. I remarked, "Sister, you seem very happy." "O yes!" she exulted. "They take such wonderful care of me here. Everyone is so kind. The food is excellent. I have lots of time to pray. God is good to me!" Here was a woman unable to walk, completely dependent on others to meet her needs, yet so gloriously happy and holy that she radiated joy to all she met.

Saint Paul, who found happiness in his union with Christ crucified, experienced even greater joy in the realization that his suffering could be a blessing, a prayer, for others: "I am now rejoicing in my sufferings for your sake, and in my flesh I am completing what is lacking in Christ's afflictions for the sake of his body, that is, the church" (Colossians 1:24). In God's plan, we can join our suffering to Jesus' to help bring his grace to people today. Christ's sufferings and death were sufficient to redeem humankind, but Christ needs the suffering members of his Body to direct his redemptive love to the world. This is something of a mystery, but it is tied to the efficacy of love. Love joins us to God, and when we offer our sufferings in union with Christ to God, we express our love for God and convey that love to others. Just as a Mother who stays up all night caring for a sick child communicates God's love to her child, so our suffering can communicate God's love to others. Marguerite, an elderly woman with diabetes was confined to bed after both legs were amputated. When asked if the days didn't seem long to her, she replied, "Not at all. The days are never long enough for me to say all the prayers I want to offer for my family and friends." Marguerite found joy, as did Saint Paul, in joining her sufferings to those of Jesus for the sake of his body, the Church.

Union with God, growth in holiness, and ministry to others are blessings brought by Jesus to those who suffer. He speaks to us the words he addressed to his apostles on the night before he died: "So you have pain now; but I will see you again, and your hearts will rejoice, and no one will take your joy from you" (John 16:22).

CHOOSING HAPPINESS IN THE FACE OF SUFFERING AND DEATH

We've all met people who smile through pain and remain serene in the face of death. We also met those who make misery for themselves and others by constant complaining about misfortunes. Happiness is always a matter of choice, as is unhappiness. But especially when difficulties cross our days must we realize that we can choose to be happy. We can make decisions that bring joy. What are these decisions?

One very important decision is to have a sense of humor. Jack Buck, the Hall of Fame announcer for the Saint Louis Baseball Cardinals, continued to work in spite of diabetes, Parkinson's disease, sciatica, and heart problems requiring a pacemaker. But instead of complaining, Jack joked about his ailments. "I wish I'd get Alzheimer's," he laughed. "Then I could forget I've got all the other stuff."

There are, after all, some benefits to growing older. When we are younger we need to be more careful about our eating habits because of long-term damage caused by some foods. But once we reach a certain age, long-term damage is no longer possible. Not long ago I was told by my doctor that I could eat anything I want because I'm as good as dead anyway!

Another key decision is to maintain a sense of balance about our problems. Ben is a former airline pilot who had to retire from flying because of numerous back surgeries. In constant pain, he never complains. After one of his many visits to the hospital he remarked, "I see those little children paralyzed in an accident or struggling with leukemia and I realize that my problems are pretty small."

I used to feel sorry for myself because arthritis kept me from active participation in some sports. Then I started visiting a parishioner with cancer of the spine. Still in his forties, he would look longingly out his bedroom window and say, "I'd give anything if I could just walk out into the yard." As I left his house and walked back to my car, albeit with a limp, arthritis didn't seem so troublesome as it had on the way in.

We can choose to see our sufferings and the problems of old age as a way to prepare for eternal life. God may give us additional years of suffering because they are needed to open us up to new possibilities for happiness in heaven. Many years ago a prison chaplain told me about a tough old jailbird, age ninety-five, he was trying to help. In response to his best efforts to tell the prisoner about the God's mercy, the old man would snarl, "All my relatives are in hell and that's where I'm going." But the chaplain persisted, and eventually the elderly prisoner was baptized. He spent his last days saying that he was looking forward to heaven. In his case, long years of suffering finally cracked the hard shell of resistance he had built around himself, and pain opened his heart to the joy of eternal life.

Sometimes patient preparation for heaven and a sense of humor go together. A gentleman who often visited the sick at a nursing home related that one resident, age ninety-seven, was wondering why she was still alive. He told her it was because God loved her and was giving her some extra time to prepare for heaven and make up for any sins she had committed. "Oh my goodness," she replied, "I'm going to live to be to be two hundred!"

TO BE HAPPY FOREVER

Many books have been written about the meaning of suffering and death. But of all the things that can be said, nothing is more important than this: Jesus Christ is a co-sufferer with us and his death and Resurrection lead us through death to eternal life. God made us to be happy forever, and death is the way to that happiness. This is not wishful thinking. It is Christ's promise: "In my Father's house there are many dwelling places. If it were not so, would I have told you that I go to prepare a place for you? And if I go and prepare a place for you, I will come again and will take you to myself, so that where I am, there you may be also" (John 14:2–3).

A mother whose young son had died of cancer said that she received a great deal of comfort from a verse sent her by a friend: "When I was born, people were happy and smiling. I was the only one crying. When I died, people were sad and crying. I was the only one smiling."

Countless near-death experiences verify the truth of these words. Jessica was badly injured in a car accident. She felt she was dying and prayed, "Whatever you want, Lord." Overwhelmed with a sense of peace, she lost consciousness. She discovered as she woke in a hospital bed that what the Lord wanted was her return to this life. But she feels blessed by the knowledge that the approach of death brought, not fear, but the confident assurance of eternal life.

We need not wait for the moment of death to place our lives in God's hands. We can say today, and every day, "Thy will be done." We can choose to accept the joy that comes from trusting in Jesus Christ: "I will see you again, and your hearts will rejoice, and no one will take your joy from you" (John 16:22).

And while we are still on this earth, we can search for happiness by developing a Christlike control of our emotions and a Christ-centered spirituality. Emotional health and spiritual growth are essential to our happiness, and we shall explore these topics in the next two chapters.

REFLECTIONS

What is your opinion of the explanation of suffering found in the section, "Why Suffering and Death?" How would you explain the existence of suffering in the world? Have you ever thought of death as birth? Consider these words: "You have already died once." What does this statement mean? Have you known people like Catherine, Cindy, Doctor Joe, and Mary Beth who have faced death with courage and hope? The section, "Meaning in Suffering," lists three blessings connected to suffering. Can you explain each of these in your own words? What is your opinion of old age? Would you rather die before experiencing the limitations of old age, or would you like more time to prepare for heaven? When you are suffering, do you try to think of Jesus as suffering with you? After reading this chapter, Kathy observed that when teaching math to a child, you don't begin with calculus. You use beads, taking away some to teach subtraction and putting some in to teach addition. So God leads us through lower levels of happiness to the highest. We begin life with a craving for food and gradually move into higher levels of happiness. At the end of life we move away from the lower levels. We lose our appetite for food. We give away the things we've accumulated. Our friends die. And we are made ready to be taken into God's loving arms. What do you think of Kathy's idea? Have you known anyone who grew closer to God as old age took away the ability to enjoy lower levels of happiness?

SIX

THE FOUR LEVELS AND EMOTIONAL HEALTH

D avid was business administrator at a parish I served as pastor. He combined a deep faith in Christ with a remarkable proficiency at his job. I admired his ability to handle stressful situations with quiet competence. He possessed a humble self-assurance that enabled him to undertake difficult projects without anxiety. He was more concerned about the needs of others than his own. He was patient, even with people who were irritating and irrational. He could be firm, but I never heard him raise his voice in anger. A man of strong feelings, he knew how to control and how to express his emotions.

If we want to be happy, we must learn to deal with our emotions. Emotions provide energy and motivation for our journey through life in much the same way as an engine provides power for an automobile. But just as the driver must control the engine, so we must control our emotions.

Uncontrolled emotions wreak havoc at every level. Anxiety and loneliness plunge some people into eating disorders, alcoholism, or drug abuse. Feelings of insecurity cause others to pile up material possessions as a way of appearing successful. Resentment and hostility keep many from loving relationships. Fear and doubt drive needy individuals from the mercy and compassion of God.

We must understand and control our emotions. In most cases, we can do this with study, discipline, and the help of God's grace. But in some circumstances, professional assistance is needed. This is certainly true when someone is afflicted with clinical depression.

CLINICAL DEPRESSION

Carol had a loving family, financial security, many friends, and a deep faith in God. But suddenly her life began to disintegrate. This is how she describes her experience:

Two weeks after the birth of my third child I started to fall apart physically, troubled by insomnia and loss of appetite. Then came emotional changes: anxiety, crying, lack of concentration. As the symptoms intensified, thoughts of suicide seeped in. I found myself drowning spiritually.

My lowest point mentally came when I couldn't prepare a box of macaroni and cheese, and physically when I couldn't get out of bed. My lowest point spiritually came when I stood in the back of the church looking at Christ on the cross and asking, "What have you done for me lately?" And this lowest point became a turning point when Jesus responded gently, to my heart, "I died for you."

I needed medical help, physical and mental assessment, therapy, and proper medication. Chemical imbalances that were at the core of my depression had to be treated and brought under control.

My husband was supportive in every way. When I woke in the middle of the night from suffocating fear, he would hold and rock me. A call to his office during his workday because I felt I couldn't keep going would bring him home immediately, again to hold me and assure me everything would be all right. Through all my months in the dark hole of depression, he remained loving and faithful.

That was fifteen years ago. The experience was painful, but it has enabled me to help others. Recently an elderly friend lost his wife and is now in the depths of depression. He is being treated by doctors who are trying to adjust his medication. He shared with me that he finds it hard to pray. I told him that in my darkest days my prayer was simply, "Jesus, be with me." Then I promised him something that was repeated to me over and over again by my doctors, my husband, my friends, and—in my heart—by God. "It will get better. It will get better." It did for me, and I am confident that it will for my friend.

The journey out of depression is not easy. It takes the grace of God, the love of family and friends, and treatment by competent physicians. Once out, maintenance with medication may be necessary. But for those in depression—I promise—it will get better.

Most of us occasionally feel sad or discouraged without being able to trace our mood to any definite cause. It is normal to have emotional peaks and valleys, and to experience mild depression for no apparent reason. We may have three or four such days a month. Eventually we learn to recognize these times and tough them out, knowing we will soon feel better. But clinical depression drags its victims to depths where it becomes impossible to do the most ordinary task, like preparing a package of macaroni and cheese. Those afflicted wonder what is wrong. Friends and family may tell them to snap out of it, to cheer up. But it is as impossible for a person with clinical depression to cheer up as it is for someone with a severed spinal cord to walk.

Recovery from clinical depression requires medical treatment, the support of family and friends, and the grace of God. With these helps, as Carol discovered, life will get better.

There are other circumstances related to emotional and physical health which require professional care. These include disabling conditions such as serious psychological illness, chemical dependency, and alcoholism. But for everyday management of our emotions, the four levels of happiness provide a pattern and guide. Here we look at those levels and examine important emotional issues involved in each.

HAPPINESS ONE AND EMOTIONAL HEALTH

There is a close relationship between bodily appetites and emotions. On the one hand hunger or thirst can make us irritable. Fatigue can cause depression. Satisfaction of bodily appetites brings happiness. On the other hand anxiety may create a craving for food or drink. Sorrow can wear down the body. Joy gives vitality and strength.

If we want to be happy, we must never allow bodily appetites to overrule mind and will. Rather, we follow the guidelines for human conduct found in the Bible. We reviewed many of these directives in Chapter One, and they must regulate our desires for food, drink, and pleasure. Giving in to unruly appetites might produce short-term gratification, but this is quickly outweighed by the damage done to body and spirit. Loss of control leads to regret, sadness, contempt of self, and many other negative emotions. Keeping mind and will in charge of appetites and emotions produces the confidence and courage needed to live effectively.

At this First Level of Happiness and at the other levels as well, we should be aware of the connection between emotions and imagination. The imagination produces "graphics" that accompany thoughts, and it can be either a dynamic servant or a merciless master. When we keep the imagination under the rule of mind and will, we have an effective God-given tool to achieve positive goals. Someone trying to diet, for example, might form an image of the ideal weight to be achieved, and let this image provide guidance and encouragement. A man tempted to commit adultery might let his imagination portray his wife and children, sheltered by the loving arms of Christ, and use this picture to block out temptation. But if the imagination is allowed to run wild, it can drag us into every kind of unhappiness. Unchecked desires for food and drink, fed by an overactive imagination, can make cravings seem overwhelming. Pornography can produce images that drive otherwise sensible people to criminal acts of rape and child abuse, blocking out positive emotions like compassion with the desire to satisfy selfish urges, no matter what the cost to others.

At this and all levels of happiness we must be aware of another quality of emotions and imagination. They tend to accelerate. They are like cars parked on level ground just above a steep hill. If a car without a driver begins to move on level ground, it can be blocked easily enough. But once it begins to rocket down the hill, it will crush anyone trying to stop it. So a temptation to illicit sexual pleasure can be readily controlled if checked at once. But if that temptation is allowed to roll along, fueled by pictures from the imagination, it will careen down to emotions and consequences that wreck happiness.

Another characteristic of emotions is that they are neutral in themselves. A feeling of fear or anger or grief may rise up unbidden with the potential to serve positively or negatively. Fear can keep us from taking foolish chances, or it can block us from saving a life. Anger can rouse us to battle against injustice, or it can lead to road rage. Grief can turn us to prayer, or sink us into despair. Emotions need guidance from the mind and direction from the will.

93

Most often the mind and will must exercise control over emotions and imagination by commands, not by reasoning. Many feelings have no basis in fact. Someone, for example, might be afraid to take an elevator. The imagination steps in with vivid pictures of shattered machinery and broken bodies. The pictures ignite the feelings, which in turn fire up the imagination. Emotions and imagination build on one another until the person is overwhelmed by fear. It doesn't matter that statistics prove elevators are safer than stairways. A fearful person can argue endlessly with wild imaginings and emotions without gaining any ground. The solution is to exercise dominion over both, step onto the elevator, and override the fear.

The body is involved in this whole process. Unfounded fears and groundless anxieties cause physical symptoms like butterflies in the stomach, wobbling knees, sweaty palms and trembling hands. In order to avoid these discomforts, some people become slaves to their runaway emotions. They may gain a very limited form of Happiness One, a temporary respite from physical distress, but in doing so they block out higher levels of happiness and allow feelings to dominate mind and will.

In a healthy person, emotions and imagination provide energy. The mind directs. The will commands. The body obeys. Meg is a young lady who plays several musical instruments and has a fine voice. She had agreed to sing solo at a church service. While visiting her family, I asked her to perform the song since I couldn't attend the service. She was very reluctant because she felt self-conscious singing for only one person. Naturally, I gave her a brief lecture on the importance of acting against fears! Finally, she consented, sang beautifully, and remarked that the incident helped her overcome her shyness. Acting against our fears is the best way to conquer them and to clear a pathway to higher levels of happiness.

HAPPINESS TWO AND EMOTIONAL HEALTH

One has only to attend a high-school sporting event to witness the lively emotions, the ecstasy, that Happiness Two can generate. But it is at this level, where we strive for success, achievement, victory, and approval, that wayward emotions have perhaps the most capacity to cause mischief. Here happiness depends largely on what people think of us and on how we compare ourselves to others. This is fertile ground for harmful feelings like envy, jealousy, resentment, inadequacy, insecurity, self-pity, anxiety, discouragement, and unjust anger.

If we depend too much on Happiness Two and on the approval of others as the measure of our self-worth, we will harbor feelings of envy, jealousy, and resentment against those who excel. Comparing ourselves to those who seem superior will weigh us down with feelings of inadequacy, insecurity, and self-pity. The prospect of competing with others will fill us with anxiety, and any failure will bring discouragement. Dwelling on the successes of those we dislike will produce unjust anger.

All these emotions have something in common. They are deadly. They take over the soul, blocking out healthy emotions and the possibility of real happiness. The antidote to such feelings is commanding them to depart and acting decisively against them. Excessive dependence on Happiness Two must be replaced by the joys that flow from higher levels of happiness.

Many years ago I celebrated a wedding for a couple who have had a very happy marriage. But at first they had to deal with a problem. The wife, a college student, had been head cheerleader, homecoming queen, and valedictorian of her high-school class. Yet she felt that she wasn't pretty or intelligent. She had almost married a scoundrel soon after high-school graduation because she thought he was the best she could hope for. Fortunately, this wedding never materialized, and a few years later she met her future husband, a gentleman ten years older than she. He helped her gain a better opinion of herself, but it took time. After their marriage, she studied constantly for college classes, always afraid she would fail even though she had a 4.0 grade point average. Finally her husband informed her that he had not married her to watch her spend the rest of her life studying. He convinced her to limit study time to one hour per class. Her grade point average remained perfect, as he had assured her it would. In time, she came to accept the fact that she was very intelligent, and beautiful too.

This process of growth was fostered by the love of husband and wife for each other and by their faith in God. Because he loved her and showed his love in many practical ways, she trusted him. In his acceptance of her, his praise of her abilities and talents, his willingness to discuss her insecurities, she found the confidence to trust in herself. Because she loved him, he wanted to grow along with her and so became more patient and understanding. Their prayer together drew them closer as a couple. It gave them strength for the present, hope for the future, and grace to overcome the past. Unhappiness Two, caused by unfounded feelings of inadequacy, vanished under the influence of Happiness Three and Four.

Insecurity is one way to let Unhappiness Two cause turmoil in our emotional life. Another is to become overly concerned about the opinions of those who are disturbed, hostile, or otherwise off-center. If we try to please people who have emotional problems, we will end up with worse problems of our own. Some people cannot be pleased or do not want to be pleased. We must recognize that they are unbalanced, and that it is impossible to appease them. A high-school candidate for homecoming queen told me she was upset because some girls were spreading rumors that faculty members favored her. As a result, if she won she'd feel bad because her enemies would claim faculty bias. If she lost she would be miserable because her enemies would rejoice in her defeat. She couldn't find happiness as long as it depended on the jealousy and pettiness of her rivals. We won't find happiness either if we let our peace of mind depend on the unreasonable attitudes of others.

A young woman said she was upset about having to return home at Christmas to visit her mother. "My mother criticizes and complains," she explained, "and she makes me feel miserable. I try to change her mind. We start arguing and get angry at each other. I love my mother and do want to visit her, but I just wish we could get along better." The young woman and I discussed the situation, especially the fact that her mother's discontent derived from unrelated personal problems. She began to realize that while her mother wasn't going to change, she didn't have to let her mother's attitude spoil her day, and she did not have to reform her mother. She went home determined to try this approach, and later reported that she'd had an enjoyable visit. She didn't overreact to her mother's complaining, tried to show some sympathy, and didn't let herself be drawn into useless arguments. It made her stay at home more pleasant, and even seemed to help her mother be a little happier.

And we must not let people control us by allowing them to hurt our feelings. A high-school girl told me in a counseling session that some other girls at school were calling her ugly. I asked the young lady, who was quite attractive, if she or her friends thought she was ugly. "No," she replied. "But I still feel awful when anybody says mean things about me." I asked her to imagine a little green frog hopping into the room and calling out to her, "You are ugly because you are not green and you don't have warts." After she stopped laughing, I asked if she'd feel bad because she wasn't green and didn't have warts. "Of course not." "Why?" "Because I don't want to look like a frog." So I pointed out that while her detractors were not frogs, they very definitely had allowed the green tinge of envy and the warts of cruelty to damage their own personalities. I suggested that she consider the source of any future attacks, and pay them as much heed as she would to the imaginary insults of the little green frog.

It was good advice. I just wish I could keep it! A few years after this incident, I preached an Easter sermon that I'd carefully prepared. Reaction was very positive, except for one hostile letter which derided the sermon as inane and silly. I discussed the letter with several people, including a deacon. They assured me that the sermon had been meaningful and the letter had no merit. One person mentioned that the letter writer had emotional problems. Nevertheless, I allowed the critic to make me feel unhappy and to rule out the positive comments of many other parishioners. It was time for me to invoke the "little green frog principle," to say a prayer for the person who had written the letter, and to forget the whole thing. I did. But it took about a month. Which means I let someone else control my feelings and restrict my happiness for that period of time.

There's another more subtle way we can allow harmful emotions to cause Unhappiness Two. It's the process of imagining that others will criticize us for something we are doing. Perhaps we take an extra week's vacation, allowed by company policy. We suspect that our boss is critical of us for this decision. So we spoil our vacation by fussing and fuming about how the boss doesn't appreciate us. We develop elaborate arguments to explain why we deserved the extra week. We wallow in self-pity about the many hours we've put in without the boss knowing of our dedication. We defend ourselves against imagined criticism. And what have we accomplished? We've produced emotional stress, caused a good deal of Unhappiness Two, and gained nothing. As likely as not, we'll discover the whole process was a waste of time. For when we return to work after vacation, armed and ready for combat, the boss will smile and say: "Great to have you back. I hope you had a wonderful vacation. I've been concerned that you were working too hard!"

We have to train ourselves to ignore any criticism that isn't reasonable, whether it comes from others or from our own imagination. When our own resources are lacking, we should turn to friends for assistance. We should think about the unjust denunciations Jesus endured. We should turn to him for the grace and strength to ignore unfounded criticism. This is not easy, but it can be done. It will bring peace to our emotional life, and Happiness Two besides.

HAPPINESS THREE AND EMOTIONAL HEALTH

Happiness Three results from our efforts to love and serve others. Any emotion that lessens love will also diminish happiness. That includes the negative emotions listed above as well as many others. Here we will focus on the one situation most injurious to Happiness Three, the inability to forgive.

When we are offended by someone, especially when the offense is grave, we are assaulted with a whole range of negative feelings like hatred, resentment, contempt, rage, and the desire for revenge. Such emotions make happiness difficult, if not impossible. They cause great harm to our mind and spirit. Medical research has shown that these feelings cause physical damage as well, like increased blood pressure, severe headaches, stomach maladies, nervous conditions, and a host of other ailments. The remedy, recommended by Jesus and modeled by him, is forgiveness of enemies.

Forgiving those who offend us when they express regret and ask for pardon may not be easy, but it is usually within our reach. With God's help we can forgive such people their trespasses because we want them, and God, to forgive ours. But when an enemy harms us and shows no sorrow or continues to injure us, forgiveness becomes very difficult indeed. What does it mean to forgive someone who doesn't ask pardon? How can we forgive those who continue to injure us? What does it mean to love our enemies?

Jim's and Rita's little daughter died when her illness was not diagnosed properly. The doctor expressed no regret, and they were unable to seek legal recourse because of circumstances beyond their control. Filled with grief, anger, resentment, and frustration, they asked how they could forgive the man who had done them such harm.

I could only respond that when Jesus tells us to forgive enemies, he does not mean we must become friends with those who hurt us. It does mean that we turn to Jesus for the grace to keep from being consumed by anger and hatred. It means we refrain from vengeful acts in an effort to get even. It means we pray for grace to overcome harsh feelings because they harm us, not the one who did the offense. It has been said that harboring hatred is like taking poison and waiting for the other person to die. If we cannot release our ill-will for the sake of our enemies, we must release it for our own sake, to free ourselves for the happiness only God can give.

This may be beyond our ability. It becomes possible by the grace of God. A prayer like the following can help us remain open to that grace:

Jesus, you know how upset we are because of the harm done to us. You forgave those who harmed you. Please help us to forgive, so that we will not be destroyed by anger, hatred, or revenge. Help those who have harmed us to follow you, so that they may not hurt others. We place ourselves in your care. Bless us with your strength and peace and love, so that what has happened to us may cause no further damage. Instead, let us grow ever stron-

ger, full of compassion and courage and hope. Give us grace to move ahead, walking always with you at our side. Amen.

Forgiveness is elusive when an enemy continues to harm us, perhaps by gossip or by rudeness or lack of consideration. A high-school girl was targeted for ridicule and slander by a clique whose members were jealous of her accomplishments. She had heard Jesus' words in Scripture, "Do not resist an evildoer. But if anyone strikes you on the right cheek, turn the other also" (Matthew 5:39). Did this mean she was to encourage the abuse of her tormenters or try to become best friends with them? Should she confront them or remain silent? Answers to such questions are never easy. But there are some basic principles that can guide us.

When Jesus tells us to turn the other cheek, he expects us to consider the circumstances. We know this because Jesus did not always turn the other cheek. When he was slapped by a temple guard during his interrogation by Annas, he confronted his persecutors (John 18:23). But when he was mocked by Herod's court, he remained silent, turning the other cheek (Luke 23:6–11). Perhaps Jesus felt his rebuke might help the temple guard to repent, whereas he knew that speaking to Herod would do no good.

So there are situations where it is best to confront those who have hurt us. Perhaps they weren't aware of the harm they caused. Perhaps they can be helped by confrontation and correction. In other cases, our best recourse is to remain silent because we might do more harm than good by bringing up the injury. In difficult situations, especially when we know the other person is not sorry and doesn't want to change, we should pray for guidance to know the best course of action. We should ask wise friends for advice.

When Christ asks us to forgive our enemies, he does not mean we should invite them to keep on hurting us. When foes are eager to continue their mischief, forgiveness does not mean reconciliation. This is impossible because the others do not want it. But we must turn to Christ for the grace to forgive and to refrain from vengeance. We must pray for our enemies, asking Jesus to help them become more like him.

In such situations we must never underestimate the power of God's grace. Ernie's granddaughter was killed by a drunken driver. Ernie was consumed with hatred, rage, and anguish. "I know I'm killing myself with these feelings," he said. "And I know they don't hurt the one who killed my granddaughter. But I just can't seem to let go of them." Eventually, however, Ernie found peace by looking at an image of Christ on the cross and pondering his words, "Father, forgive them; for they do not know what they are doing" (Luke 23:34).

Some time ago I read about a woman whose son was killed by a drunken driver, a young man from a dysfunctional family. He was convicted and put in prison. The woman turned to Jesus for the help she needed to forgive. She began to visit the young man in prison, and when he was released, she took him into her own home. God's grace enabled her to do what might have been humanly impossible. Her willingness to forgive brought happiness to her and to the one forgiven.

At times our hurt may be so deep that we need to seek out a spiritual guide such as a pastor or Christian counselor to help us talk out our pain and enter a path toward forgiveness. Through loving people who know how to listen and to advise, Jesus eases the pain of loss, teaches us to forgive, and brings peace.

When hatred and anger create a chasm between us and the happiness we long for, Jesus can bridge the gap. When ungovernable feelings destroy peace of mind, making us incapable of love or the joy love alone can bring, Jesus is our strength. In our efforts to achieve Happiness Three and the positive emotions that flow from it, the words of Saint Paul must be our guide: "I can do all things through him who strengthens me" (Philippians 4:13).

HAPPINESS FOUR
AND EMOTIONAL GROWTH

When I met the young lady who had a low opinion of herself in spite of her many accomplishments, I thought the situation was unusual. But I've since discovered that her problem was anything but unique. One woman I admired very much as an ideal wife and mother stunned me during an appointment when she broke down crying because she felt she was a failure. I've met many teenagers who wished they were more talented or better looking or more intelligent, even though they were admired by their peers. It's amazing how many people feel inferior to others, who in turn feel inferior to the ones who put them on a pedestal. Even the wealthy and famous experience feelings of mediocrity and inadequacy. Many professional athletes, movie stars, and other public figures try to drown their insecurity with alcohol or deaden it with drugs.

Today's world doesn't offer much help. We are often reduced to statistics or marketing pawns. Advertising makes us feel our teeth aren't bright enough, our deodorant is letting us down, and our clothes are hopelessly outdated. We know we'll never be as handsome or as beautiful as the actors on the screen. They won't either, because they depend on makeup artists, and they feel inferior because they know the person portrayed by the camera bears no resemblance to who they really are.

The solution for all feelings of inferiority can be found in God. The Maker of the universe loves us as dear children. Jesus values us so highly that he gave his life for us on the cross. The Holy Spirit considers us worthy of loving union. In the assurance of God's love for us, in Happiness Four, we find a remedy for feelings of inadequacy and inferiority. We find the security and assurance to reach out to others as Jesus did.

Happiness Four, knowing and loving God, can provide emotional strength, peace of heart, and courage of spirit when it includes a firm trust in God's Providence. God created all things, and God's Providence rules over creation. This means that nothing can happen without God's willing or allowing it. The saints accepted good and bad, joyful successes and unavoidable setbacks because they believed these were part of God's plan. They realized that evil is the sad consequence of sin and human weakness, not willed by God, but allowed for the sake of human freedom. They knew, however, that God could bring good out of evil, that suffering united them to Jesus, and that even death would be turned to eternal life. As a result, they did all they could to eradicate the causes and effects of sin in the world, but they maintained peace of mind and a resolute courage in every circumstance.

Mother Teresa lived in the midst of terrible suffering, but brought joy to all she met. She knew she could not change the whole world, but she served Christ with every ounce of her strength against overwhelming odds. When confronted with the criticism that she could reach only a small percentage of the needy people on earth, she replied that God does not ask us to be successful, but faithful. And she kept doing her work for the poor.

Living under the wings of God's providential care means that we pray often the words of Jesus, "Thy will be done," and try to live by them. There is no better road to peace of soul than to accept God's will in every circumstance. "Thy will be done" should be our prayer when beginning a task, when meeting with success, when dealing with failure, and when facing the unknown. Robert was a physician who devoted his life to healing the sick and serving worthwhile causes. He retired and moved to Montana to enjoy time with family members who lived there. But soon afterward he was diagnosed with bone cancer that put an end to his hopes for a pleasant retirement. I spoke with him several times and was impressed by his faith and acceptance of God's will. On one occasion he remarked: "God doesn't owe me anything. I've had more blessings than I can ever repay. I'd like a few more years, but whatever God wishes is fine. I only want what God wants."

All too often my own approach is: "I want what God wants, provided God wants what I do. Not thy will, but mine be done." It's easy to see my own requests as matters involving just God and me. But God must fit my wishes and decisions into a pattern that includes all the wishes and decisions of six billion other people, some of whom are deliberately trying to thwart God's will. Our world is like a giant jigsaw puzzle of six billion living pieces constantly changing shape and location. This living puzzle has been in the process of formation for hundreds of thousands of years, and will not be completed until the end of time. Only God can fit my life into such a pattern. I cannot. I must learn to trust.

Whatever God wills is best. This is easier to say than to believe. As I look back over the years, I recall many circumstances that seemed unpleasant and disruptive. I did more than my share of complaining about them. But out of these circumstances came blessings I could never have foreseen. And so I try to learn from past mistakes. I strive often to say and to mean the words Jesus taught and lived: "Thy will be done."

Trust in God's Providence helps us overcome a common source of unhappiness, useless regret. "If only" is a deadly phrase when it makes us agonize over past events. "If only I had left ten minutes earlier, I would have avoided that accident." "If only I had not let my son play football, he would not have been injured." "If only she had taken a later flight, she would still be with us." We cannot change the past, and reliving circumstances that cannot be altered is a sure path to misery. We must put the past in God's hands, live in the present, and do what we can to make the future better.

"Where did I go wrong?" is another expression that should usually be replaced with an act of trust in God. If someone has done wrong, that person should review the past. Drunken drivers should ponder any harm they have done, make amends, and take steps to change. But many people blame themselves endlessly without cause. Parents often accuse themselves when an adult child turns away from Christ. They may have done their best, and their child is responsible for any misdeed. Jesus is not to be blamed for the sins of Judas, and parents who have tried to raise their children properly should not blame themselves for the failures of their children.

"Why me?" is another route to unhappiness, self-pity, and useless discontent. We should ask, "Why not me?" We must accept the fact that in an imperfect world misfortune can come our way. We must trust that God will be able to bring good out of any distress. We must turn to God for the help we need to move ahead with courage. A severe rainstorm caused flooding and severe damage in a Southeast Missouri shopping center. I was impressed by the courage of friends whose business was devastated by the high water. They could have said, "Why me?" "It isn't fair." "If only we had located elsewhere...." Instead they said, "We'll clean up and carry on. God kept us safe. We can replace the things that were destroyed."

ROMANS 8 AND SERENITY

Taking charge of our emotional life takes time. Once when I complimented David, the parish administrator mentioned at the beginning of this chapter, for handling a difficult situation very calmly, he replied, "You should have known me twenty years ago! Learning to control my emotions took a lot of time and the grace of God." As we strive to put our feelings at the service of mind, will, and soul, there are two resources that are especially helpful: the absolute assurance that God is in charge, and turning to God often in prayer.

There is no greater assurance than that found in Romans 8:38–39. "For I am convinced that neither death, nor life, nor angels, nor rulers, nor things present, nor things to come, nor powers, nor height, nor depth, nor anything else in all creation, will be able to separate us from the love of God in Christ Jesus our Lord."

A fine way to petition God for peace of soul is the Serenity Prayer: *Lord, grant me the serenity to accept the things I cannot change, the courage to change the things I can, and the wisdom to know the difference.*

And our emotional life will be all the stronger when it is fortified by a strong spiritual life, as we shall see in Chapter Seven.

REFLECTIONS

Have you known people like David who impressed you with their ability to control and express their emotions? Some people who have undergone severe depression say that friends give advice like "Just cheer up" or "Put your trust in God." Why is such advice defective? What kind of advice would you give to a person suffering clinical depression? This chapter includes considerations of emotional health as related to each of the four levels of happiness. What did you find most helpful in each of the four sections? Which statements do you find questionable? What does forgiveness of enemies mean to you when an apology is made, and when there is no apology? What does trust in God's Providence mean to you? Jesus' words, "Thy will be done," place our life and its circumstances in God's hands. How often do you pray these words? Have you ever thought of your wishes and decisions as parts of a constantly changing puzzle that only God can fit together? Does this notion change the way you view prayer?

SEVEN

THE FOUR LEVELS AND SPIRITUAL GROWTH

I n a retirement home for clergy, Father John, in the early stages of Alzheimer's disease, was wandering around on the third floor. When asked by another resident what he was looking for, he replied, "I'm trying to find my room." "You are on the wrong floor," he was told. "Your room is on the second floor, just below this one." Father John, who retained his sense of humor even when confused, shrugged his shoulders and quipped, "I guess I'll have to get my altimeter fixed."

Because of Adam and Eve, we all have to get our spiritual altimeters fixed. We have to raise our minds and hearts to God. Spirituality, spiritual growth, means addressing that part of ourselves that hungers for happiness, truth, beauty, goodness, eternal values. Spirituality means putting our lives in order. True spirituality directs us to give God the first place and love of others the next, then to arrange everything else after these two great priorities. This, of course, parallels the four levels of happiness.

Today's world of rapid transportation and instant communication keeps us running at a frantic pace. We give time to those things which seem most important or require immediate attention. Spirituality may not seem as pressing or significant as preparing the next meal, paying the bills, or attending a business meeting.

But if we understand that happiness, something we all want,

is intimately linked with spirituality, we may discover the motivation needed to pursue both spirituality and happiness with new enthusiasm. If we realize that the four levels of happiness provide a pattern for putting our lives in order, we will attain not only happiness, but a practical spirituality and a genuine holiness as well.

What we have considered up to this point is closely connected with spirituality. We have looked at life's great question, "Why are we here?" and its answer, "to know, love, and serve God, and to be happy forever." We saw how God's original plan for our happiness was set aside by Adam and Eve. Created to enjoy union with God, love of others, achievement, and physical pleasure, they rejected love of God and one another. As a consequence, we find ourselves in a maze where sensual pleasure and egoism override reason, push God into the background, and tempt us to trample others underfoot. Hopelessly lost in this condition of sin, we are shown a path to safety in Scripture and rescued by the life, death, and Resurrection of Jesus. In Jesus and in the Bible, especially the Ten Commandments, we discover a map that guides us through successive levels of happiness, guards us from corresponding levels of unhappiness, and leads us ultimately to the One who alone can fulfill all our desires.

In this chapter we will spotlight several foundational themes of Christianity that associate spirituality and happiness. We will consider ways to allow God to grace our lives and influence how we think, speak, and act. In short, we will fix our spiritual altimeters.

THE TRINITY AND THE TWO GREAT COMMANDMENTS

From all eternity, God exists as a community of Persons—Father, Son, and Holy Spirit—a community of perfect love. "God is love" (1 John 4:16). God created us in time with the ability to love. God the Son entered our human family, brought us a new awareness of God's love and touched us with it. "For it is the God who said, 'Let light shine out of darkness,' who has shone in our hearts to give the light of the knowledge of the glory of God in the face of Jesus Christ" (2 Corinthians 4:6).

It is no surprise, then, that when Jesus was asked for the greatest commandment, he replied: "You shall love the Lord your God with all your heart, and with all your soul, and with all your mind" (Matthew 22:37). He immediately added the second: "You shall love your neighbor as yourself" (Matthew 22:39). These two commandments sum up the law and teaching of Scripture, and they point the way to true happiness.

Spirituality, therefore, involves loving union, friendship, with God. We know God as a loving Father, as Jesus our Brother who died for us, as Holy Spirit and Guest of our souls. It might seem difficult to imagine that friendship can be possible between ourselves and the Creator of a universe thirty billion light-years across. But both the Old Testament (Exodus 33:11) and the New (John 15:15) present such friendship as a reality. So we should wonder: "If I were asked for a list of my best friends, would God be right at the top?"

If not, we need a reality check! The God who created us, who died on the cross for us, and who will judge us at the moment of death asks for our friendship. When we consider how much happiness we receive from human relationships, we should be overwhelmed at the joy possible through friendship with God.

Once we realize that we are invited to be friends of God, where do we begin? How does a creature relate to the Creator? One way is to examine what is involved in human friendships. *We are attentive to friends. We spend time with them. We listen to them. We express our love for them, esteem their goodness, and admire their accomplishments. We are grateful for their kindnesses toward us. If we offend them in any way, we are quick to apologize. We request assistance from friends. We are eager to assist them. We treat their loved ones with regard. We respect their opinions. We want to be close to friends, to be one with them.*

These elements of human friendship provide a blueprint for building our friendship with God. They find expression in our communication with God, in prayer. We may mistakenly think of prayer only as asking. But just as asking is only a small part of conversing with others, so it is only a limited part of prayer. Prayer includes adoring God as Creator of the universe, thanking God for blessings, and asking forgiveness for sins. Such prayer unfailingly unites us to God. Once we realize this and see prayer as union with God, we discover…

PRAYER THAT NEVER FAILS

Attentiveness to God. We are never far from God. God sustains us in existence, and without God we would cease to be. "In him we live and move and have our being" (Acts 17:28). But it is one thing to be with a person, and another to be attentive. At times we can be so preoccupied with other things that we fail to notice those we love.

So prayer begins with an effort to be more attentive to God throughout the day. We say hello to God as we rise from sleep. We acknowledge God's artistry in a beautiful sunrise. We seek guidance in a difficult decision. We whisper a prayer for patience when a coworker annoys us. We lie down to rest knowing that our lives are in God's care. This is what the great spiritual writers call "living in the presence of God."

There are many ways to be with God in our daily activities. Mike, a salesman, turns off the car radio as he drives to appointments. He pictures Jesus sitting in the passenger seat and discusses work, family, and anything else of concern. Rob, on his day off, says, "I'm going to the mountains to fly fish and to talk to God." Michelle, as she cares for her infant, remembers that Jesus identifies himself with her child. Every moment with her baby is time with Jesus (Matthew 25:40).

Spending time with God. We schedule time to be with friends, to visit, to share a meal, to celebrate special occasions. So we need to set aside time with God. Some people do this first thing in the morning, others at noon, others in the evening. The important thing is to have a prayer time and be faithful to it. If we feel this is impossible because we are just too busy, we should think about the human being we most admire and love. If this individual offered to spend fifteen minutes or half an hour with us each day, we would make room on our schedule. The Creator of the universe wishes to visit with us each day. We must find time!

Listening to God. When we are with friends, we listen to what they have to say. Listening is an essential part of prayer. God speaks to us through Scripture. Because God is not limited by time or space, God speaks to us as surely as to Moses, Isaiah, Matthew, and Paul. When we open the Bible, we dial God's number. God speaks to us also through the teaching of the Church (see Luke 10:16), the events of our lives, the beauty of creation, and the words and actions of good people.

Expressing love, esteem, admiration. After listening to God, we respond. We express our love, esteem, and admiration. This is adoration, prayer that never fails to unite us to God and bring happiness. "Praise the Lord! Praise the Lord from the heavens; praise him in the heights!" (Psalm 148:1). Scripture sings the praises of God, and we have new reasons to join the song. Recent discoveries in astronomy, physics, and microbiology, mentioned in Chapter Four, demonstrate the spectacular nature of God's accomplishments. Baseball fans jump out of their seats when a home run wins the game. An audience applauds a fine performance at the theater. God's accomplishments go far beyond anything achieved in any stadium or auditorium. When we consider what scientists are saying about the universe, about a drop of water, about any cell in our bodies, we should be in awe. A few years ago, I explained to an eighth grade class at our parish school how the universe displays God's greatness. We talked about the excitement shown by folks at sporting events and decided that God deserved a few rounds of applause. So the class organized a pep rally for the Lord. Cheerleaders developed new routines for God and led the school in one of the loudest and most enjoyable hours of praise I've ever experienced. Our own efforts at praise might be quieter, but they should be no less enthusiastic.

Here we might recognize the true purpose of praise. God does not benefit from our acclaim. We do. People who appreciate a magnificent painting are enriched by its beauty. Football fans dance for joy when their team wins the Super Bowl. When we appreciate the artwork of God's creation, we are enriched beyond measure. When we recall Christ's victory over sin and death at his Resurrection, we should sing our "Alleluias" with enthusiasm. We should experience Happiness Four.

Scripture links praise with happiness. "I will be glad and exult in you; / I will sing praise to your name, O Most High" (Psalm 9:2). "My soul magnifies the Lord, / and my spirit rejoices in

God my Savior" (Luke 1:46). A real awareness of God's greatness will help us do the same.

Gratitude. Gratitude is an essential component of prayer that never fails to bring happiness. We are quick to thank friends for favors. Recognizing the gifts we receive from others and appreciating their generosity can warm our hearts. When we take time to count God's blessings and thank God for them, we are filled with the radiance of God's goodness. "O give thanks to the LORD, for he is good, / for his steadfast love endures forever" (Psalm 136:1). Recognizing our blessings and thanking God for them is a second prayer pathway to Happiness Four.

Many years ago I visited a family of eight at Christmastime. All six children were cranky with chicken pox but were also very excited about the holidays. I asked the mother what I should preach about at Christmas. She replied, with a weary smile, "Something that makes us appreciate our blessings." In sickness and in health, gratitude is possible and it will always bring happiness. As Saint Paul wrote: "Rejoice always...give thanks in all circumstances" (1 Thessalonians 5:16).

Apologizing, seeking forgiveness. A third pathway to Happiness Four is willingness to recognize our failings and express sorrow for them. If we, in a moment of weakness, offend a good friend, we are quick to apologize as soon as we realize what we have done. Most of us have had the experience of causing pain to someone we love, asking pardon, and receiving forgiveness. Apologies, sincerely given and generously accepted, can strengthen a friendship and turn hurt to happiness. This is true in our relationship with God. "The LORD is merciful and gracious, / slow to anger and abounding in steadfast love" (Psalm 103:8). God's compassion turns the sorrow of our sinfulness into the joy of being forgiven. "Happy are those whose transgression is forgiven, /

whose sin is covered" (Psalm 32:1). A sincere act of repentance is one more prayer that never fails to bring happiness.

Requesting assistance. No one likes to ask for help, but there is a sense of quiet satisfaction in knowing friends so devoted that we can ask with confidence in time of need. There is real happiness in having our request granted, or in learning that our friends can suggest a better answer to our need. God is a Friend so devoted that Jesus encourages us to ask with confidence. "So I say to you, Ask, and it will be given you; search, and you will find; knock, and the door will be opened for you" (Luke 11:9). God is a Friend so wise that Jesus himself prayed, "Not my will but yours be done" (Luke 22:42). Praying in Jesus' name, that is, with complete confidence that God knows what is best for us and will do what is best for us, is yet another form of prayer that never fails to bring happiness.

OUR FATHER

For Christians, the prayer which surpasses all others is the one Jesus teaches in his Sermon on the Mount (Matthew 6:9–13). In this prayer we adore, thank, ask pardon, and seek assistance. When we consider the Lord's Prayer in light of the four levels of happiness, we gain a new appreciation for its depth of meaning and its capacity to impart joy.

Our Father. God is addressed as a Father who gave us life so that we might find happiness forever in God's presence. We are God's beloved children. God sees the image of Jesus in us when we pray in his words. Happiness Four finds expression in the word *Father.* And we pray not as individuals, but as members of God's family. We are joined to brothers and sisters throughout the world who pray in these same words. We are one with the whole human family. We experience Happiness Three as we say *Our* Father.

Who art in heaven. Heaven is where God is, everywhere. We should say these words with awe as we reflect on the vastness and magnificence of the created universe. The more we learn about the wonders uncovered by astronomers, microbiologists, and other scientists, the more we should feel privileged to speak to the Maker of the heavens.

Hallowed be thy name. Fans at a football or basketball game chant the name of a favorite player. They show appreciation for the athlete's talents and share in his accomplishments by their applause. When we pray the Lord's Prayer, we join the applause of those in heaven and on earth. There is much joy to be had as we step into this great circle in praise of God's name.

Thy kingdom come. We pray that people on earth may accept God's rule and priorities. In the marvelous constitution of God's kingdom, found in the teachings of Scripture and the Church, we rediscover the pathway to happiness lost by Adam and Eve.

Thy will be done on earth as it is in heaven. Jesus did not just teach us to say these words. He said them when faced with the horror of his passion and death. What God wants is best. Even in a world where people can do what God doesn't want, God can bring good from evil, light from darkness, resurrection from every cross. God, who created a hundred billion galaxies with a word, fits all human choices, good and bad, into a plan designed to give happiness to all who rely on Providence. So we pray that we may follow God's will as do those in heaven. We trust in the power of God's will to bring peace and joy to us, as it has to the angels and saints.

Give us this day our daily bread. God has given us our bodily appetites and knows our earthly needs. We entrust the fulfillment of these needs to God, thereby asking God to give us Happiness

One. Our daily bread includes also the spiritual blessings for which we hunger, especially the Bread that is Christ. And so we pray for Happiness Four.

And forgive us our trespasses as we forgive those who trespass against us. We acknowledge the sins and failings that bring us unhappiness at every level. We recognize that we can receive God's forgiveness only if we forgive others. In forgiving others, we open doors to Happiness Three and allow God to grant us the Happiness Four gifts of pardon and peace.

And lead us not into temptation... This traditional English translation seems to imply that God could lead us into temptation and thus into sin. But God does not tempt us to sin. A more accurate wording might be "Do not let us surrender to temptation." We ask God to save us from sin that falsely promises happiness but brings only misery.

...but deliver us from evil. Evil and unhappiness entered our world through the tempting of the evil one, Satan. We ask God for the strength and wisdom needed to conquer the sad lies of Satan and to live in the joyous realm of God's grace and peace.

I was making hospital visits and stopped at Barbara's room. She was seated near the window, reading. Wearing makeup and an attractive dress, she seemed more ready for a party than for medical care. But she was in the hospital to be treated for cancer, which she had been battling for four years. She proudly displayed pictures of her husband and four children, then shared her story. Over a period of forty-eight months, she had gone through four surgeries, radiation, and chemotherapy. When asked how she managed to be so cheerful and upbeat, she replied: "My faith is the most important reason. When I discovered I had cancer, I sat down and thought things out. I was sure that God would not send such an illness as punishment, and I knew God was with me. I realized that no one had promised me a garden of roses, and nowhere in the Bible was I told that life would be easy. I thought about how I felt around people who were sad and despondent, and I didn't want my illness to be a burden for my children or cause them to grow into unhappy adults. So I stay cheerful by turning to God in prayer, especially the Our Father. I don't rattle through the prayer, but say the words slowly and reflect on them one by one. When I have a painful treatment, like bone marrow removal, I don't ask for medication, but concentrate on the Our Father, word by word."

Barbara knew the power of the Lord's Prayer to impart happiness in extremely difficult circumstances. For Barbara, God was a Father whose heaven encompassed not just the distant galaxies, but her own heart. She believed God loved her dearly, and his name was precious as her source of courage and strength. She wanted God's kingdom of love and peace for her children and all those she knew. She accepted God's will, as did Jesus in the Garden of Gethsemane. She trusted in God to supply her needs, not just bread, but the spiritual and physical resources required to continue her battle against illness. She held no grudges against God or people who enjoyed good health. She forgave and knew forgiveness. She trusted that God would be with her in her illness and was not afraid of death, for God would surely deliver her from all evil.

Barbara taught me more about the Lord's Prayer than I've ever learned from any theological treatise or Bible commentary. Such books may be helpful, but they pale in comparison to the Gospel shining in the life of a woman who knew what it was to suffer with Jesus and to pray in the words Jesus had taught her.

HAPPINESS IN SERVING GOD

We are eager to assist friends. We treat their loved ones with regard. These elements of human friendship apply also to our relationship with God. This is why Jesus joins together the love of God and neighbor. "The commandment we have from him is this: those who love God must love their brothers and sisters also" (1 John 4:21). A spirituality built on the teachings of Jesus will reach out to the poor and disadvantaged because Jesus did. He said of himself: "The Spirit of the Lord is upon me, / because he has anointed me / to bring good news to the poor" (Luke 4:18). Our spirituality, our love of God, will find expression in our desire to serve the poor. "Religion that is pure and undefiled before God, the Father, is this: to care for orphans and widows in their distress, and to keep oneself unstained by the world" (James 1:27).

"Happy are those who are kind to the poor" (Proverbs 14:21). Saint Paul addressed those he served as "my joy and crown" (Philippians 4:1). Being a servant of God, helping others in Christ's name, is a source of joy—Happiness Three and Happiness Four. Mother Teresa demonstrated this to the world. But countless others have discovered the same truth. Charlene was a successful business manager for many years before retiring with her husband to a small town in central Louisiana. At first she felt lonely and unsatisfied, so she decided to volunteer at her local parish church. When I met her, she wore a constant smile and said she had never been happier. Serving others in Christ's name had brought fulfillment and joy.

There should be no surprise here, for we have seen that caring about others and loving God bring happiness. What is surprising is the next aspect of Christian spirituality, the Beatitudes. These remarkable statements made by Jesus in his Sermon on the Mount tell us that happiness can be found in unexpected places.

THE BEATITUDES

We respect their opinions. The opinions of Jesus about life and happiness are found most dramatically in the Beatitudes. Beatitude means happiness or bliss. When Jesus declares, "Blessed are the poor in spirit," he is saying, "Happy are the poor in spirit." Scholars tell us that the Greek word translated as "blessed" means something like "favored by God." This surely includes happiness, for Jesus bids us to "rejoice and be glad, for your reward is great in heaven." The Beatitudes, therefore, are Christ's guidelines for true and lasting joy, happiness now and forever. If we want to be happy, we should consider the Beatitudes (Matthew 5:3–11), and to understand them, we must view them through the prism of the life of Jesus.

Blessed are the poor in spirit, for theirs is the kingdom of heaven. The poor in spirit are those who recognize their utter dependence on God, and glory in the knowledge that their lives are in God's hands. On the cross, Jesus completely submitted his human life to God: "Father, into your hands I commend my spirit" (Luke 23:46). We must place our lives in God's hands, for we need God.

Michael is a successful businessman and a devoted husband and father. But his many duties have kept him constantly on the move. One night he was awakened by the insistent sobbing of his two-year-old son. Already exhausted by too much work and not enough sleep, Michael picked up his son and walked the floor, trying to comfort the boy in any way he could. Nothing worked. Finally, Michael broke down and wept, telling God, "You've got to help me. I just can't handle this any more." Suddenly his son stopped crying, put both hands on Michael's cheeks, then patted him on the shoulder. For Michael this was a powerful spiritual experience of the presence and grace of God. When we, like

Michael, experience our need for God, this Beatitude speaks to us. *Blessed are the poor in spirit.*

Blessed are those who mourn, for they will be comforted. As Jesus wept over Jerusalem (Luke 19:41–44), those who mourn grieve over the world's sin and injustice. As Jesus wept over the death of Lazarus (John 11), so we mourn the loss of loved ones. In Jesus we are comforted.

Jesus might give us a deep sense of peace at prayer. Or he might touch us in unexpected ways. Janet was very close to her grandmother, spent a great deal of time with her, and cared for her as she grew older. Janet inherited from her grandmother a love of flowers and had planted in her own garden bulbs from her grandmother's favorite flower, a black iris. Each year the iris would bloom in Janet's garden and in her grandmother's, a symbol of the love they shared. When Janet's grandmother died suddenly early one spring, Janet was heartbroken. The day after the funeral Janet sat at her window, praying, still sad at the loss of the dear lady who had meant so much to her. Then she noticed that the black irises were blooming, more than a month early. Wondering if the irises were a sign from God that her grandmother was enjoying new life in heaven, Janet drove through town looking for another iris. She found none. But she still finds consolation and comfort at the bouquet that spoke to her of God's love and gift of new life. *Blessed are they who mourn.*

Blessed are the meek, for they will inherit the earth. Meekness is not weakness, but a calm strength and serene self-control in the face of trouble. It took incredible strength for Jesus to humble himself to the point of accepting death on the cross. It takes strength for us to be meek in imitation of Jesus.

One afternoon I was talking with Jerry while he worked in his yard. He went to a bush in the front and scooped up a good deal of something unpleasant. "Where does that come from?" I asked. "It's the next-door neighbor's dog," Jerry replied. "Bob takes the dog for a walk every morning, and my bush is the dog's first stop." "That's really inconsiderate," I exclaimed. "Why do you put up with it?" "Well," Jerry answered, "Bob is a good neighbor in every other way, and if cleaning up after a dog is all it takes for me to keep the peace, it's no big deal." I've always admired the strength of Jerry's meekness, and it really did allow him to inherit the earth. A full-scale war over the dog's leavings would have made the block unlivable. Jerry's attitude allowed him and his family to enjoy their neighborhood. *Blessed are the meek.*

Blessed are those who hunger and thirst for righteousness, for they will be filled. Jesus so hungered for righteousness that he died to make us holy in God's sight. We emulate Jesus when we work for peace and justice.

Bill and Mary Frances have a great love for the poor. In their wedding invitations they wrote that God had blessed them with love and they wanted to share that love. They expressed their desire to distribute all wedding gifts to the needy, and requested that the gifts be suitable for the needs of the poor. Twenty years later, Bill and Mary Frances are directing a program that serves the poor, and God has taken care of their own needs as well. *Blessed are those who hunger and thirst for righteousness.*

Blessed are the merciful, for they will receive mercy. Jesus was so merciful that he forgave even those who crucified him. We find happiness in forgiving others and in bearing their shortcomings with compassion.

J. Neville Ward's book, *Five for Sorrow, Ten for Joy* presents an extraordinary example of mercy, a prayer found written on a piece of wrapping paper in Ravensbruck, a Nazi concentration camp for women, when it was liberated:

O Lord, remember not only the men and women of good will, but also those of ill will. But do not remember all the suffering they have inflicted on us. Remember the fruits we brought, thanks to this suffering: our comradeship, our loyalty, our humility, the courage, the generosity, the greatness of heart which has grown out of this; and when they come to judgment, let all the fruits that we have borne be their forgiveness (p. 63).

Blessed are the merciful.

Blessed are the pure in heart, for they will see God. Christ's heart was utterly pure. He saw all things as they truly are before God. Our hearts are pure to the extent that we see God, others, and all creation through the eyes of Jesus. This can be difficult, but when we see as Jesus does, we discover joy.

After a long series of personal, family, and financial problems, Kenneth, a young husband with two small children, learned to see through the eyes of Jesus. Explaining this new vision, he wrote: "I thought I loved my wife, but it was only if she would be the kind of person I wanted. I saw my kids as interruptions and inconveniences. How could I have been so blind? Now, knowing Jesus' love, I have peace, no matter what the future holds. I really do love Jesus. I'm going to love others, my family, friends, and the people I work with in my profession, whether or not they respond." *Blessed are the pure in heart.*

Blessed are the peacemakers, for they will be called children of God. Christ is our peace (Ephesians 2:14). World peace, the pursuit of justice and the absence of war, is a goal we long for. But it did not exist in Jesus' time, and it seems elusive in ours. Nevertheless, we can have peace with God, peace in our relationships with others, and peace of soul. Through Jesus, "God was pleased to reconcile to himself all things, whether on earth or in heaven, by making peace through the blood of his cross" (Colossians 1:20).

Bob was a successful businessman and the father of a large

family. But he became addicted to alcohol and caused years of turmoil for his wife, seven children, and business partners. Finally, divorced from his wife and alienated from his children, he checked into a clinic where he regained control of his life. He turned to Jesus for strength and guidance. His children, now adults, had been deeply affected by his many years of alcoholism and had problems relating to one another. Bob prayed for their healing and started trying to repair the damage he had done. About a year later he participated in a family gathering where he noticed that all seven children were again communicating. Soon after, Bob had lunch with a daughter who had been especially unfriendly to him. She said that for years she resented him because of his alcoholism, but now for some unknown reason her hostility had disappeared. Bob knows the reason. He gives all the credit to Jesus for healing his family and restoring peace.

Bob wanted to bring peace to his family, torn by strife of his own making. With Jesus, he became a peacemaker. He now feels reconciled with those he had hurt so badly, and he once again experiences the joy of being a child of God. *Blessed are the peacemakers.*

Blessed are those who are persecuted for righteousness' sake, for theirs is the kingdom of heaven. Blessed are you when people revile you and persecute you and utter all kinds of evil against you falsely on my account. Rejoice and be glad, for your reward is great in heaven, for in the same way they persecuted the prophets who were before you. This is surely the most difficult of the Beatitudes to accept. But if we tremble at the idea of persecution, we are in good company. Jesus sweated blood at the prospect of his passion and death, but persevered because he knew the blessedness that would follow. So we look to Jesus, "who for the sake of the joy that was set before him endured the cross, disregarding its shame, and has taken his seat at the right hand of the throne of God" (Hebrews 12:2). Martyrs from Stephen onward have looked to Jesus at God's right hand (Acts 7:55) and found joy in suffering persecution for Jesus' sake.

During the worst years of the Communist oppression of Lithuania, a group of Christians began to publish an underground newspaper, *The Chronicles,* to document the persecution of religion in their country and to inform the world of Communist oppression. In 1972, one of the editors, a young woman named Nijole Sadunaite was arrested and put on trial. Facing a long prison sentence under horrifying conditions, Nijole told her judges that Christians had committed no crime, but that the government was guilty of tyranny and disregard of human rights. She then said to them, "I love you as if you were my brothers and sisters, and I would not hesitate to give my life for any one of you." She closed with the stirring words: "This is the happiest day of my life.... We have to condemn evil as severely as possible, but we must love the person, even if he is wrong. And we can learn to do this in the school of Jesus Christ, who is our Way, our Truth, and our Life" (*The Mirror,* Diocese of Springfield-Cape Girardeau, November 4, 1977).

We cannot but marvel at such courage and love, and at how the words of Jesus have been proven true again and again. *Blessed are those who are persecuted.*

CLOSE TO THE SPIRIT

We want to be close to friends, to be one with them. Most Christians find it easy to relate to God the Father and to Jesus, but we may find it more difficult to feel close to the Holy Spirit. While we are familiar with fatherhood and know Jesus as our brother, the Holy Spirit may seem beyond our reach. But any spirituality that seeks the happiness for which God made us, Happiness Four, must be attentive to the Holy Spirit. For the Holy Spirit is as close to us as our own life spirit.

On the night before he died, Jesus promised to send the Holy Spirit as an Advocate, a Helper, who would remind us of all Jesus taught (John 14:16–26). Jesus sends the Holy Spirit upon us at baptism (Acts 2:38), and we become temples of the Holy Spirit (1 Corinthians 6:19). The Holy Spirit lives in us (2 Timothy 1:14). In company with this Guest of our souls, we find joy. Jesus himself rejoiced in the Holy Spirit (Luke 10:21). The first Christians lived "in the comfort of the Holy Spirit" (Acts 9:31) and "were filled with joy and with the Holy Spirit" (Acts 13:52).

The Holy Spirit dwells within us to open our hearts to Happiness Four. The Holy Spirit enables us to know God as Father. "For all who are led by the Spirit of God are children of God.... When we cry, 'Abba! Father!' it is that very Spirit bearing witness with our spirit that we are children of God" (Romans 8:14, 16).

The Holy Spirit empowers us with the faith to believe in Jesus as our Lord and God. "No one can say 'Jesus is Lord' except by the Holy Spirit" (1 Corinthians 12:3). Our relationship with Jesus is made possible by our divine Advocate, our Helper.

The Holy Spirit makes it possible for us to enjoy Happiness Three to the fullest possible extent. Love is the greatest gift of the Holy Spirit, and all the beautiful qualities of God's own love are shared with us through the Spirit (1 Corinthians 12:31—13:13).

THE FRUIT OF THE SPIRIT

A New Testament passage that can help us appreciate the relationship between the Holy Spirit and our own happiness is Saint Paul's description of the "fruit of the Spirit." Paul first tells us to avoid the works of the flesh, namely "fornication, impurity, licentiousness, idolatry, sorcery, enmities, strife, jealousy, anger, quarrels, dissensions, factions, envy, drunkenness, carousing, and things like these" (Galatians 5:19–21). These "works" are recipes for unhappiness at every level.

In contrast with these pathways to grief, Paul says that "the fruit of the Spirit is love, joy, peace, patience, kindness, generosity, faithfulness, gentleness, and self-control" (Galatians 5:22–23). These qualities, these virtues, result from a life of union with the Holy Spirit and so are called fruit, or fruits, of the Spirit. When we study them we cannot help but be attracted to their beauty. And if we think about really happy people we have known, we will recognize the fruits of the Spirit in them.

Love. Ron regularly hugs his grandchildren and asks, "What do you know for sure?" They've learned from him the answer: "Grandpa loves me." Four women, good friends, took a weekend together in a large city to attend a musical and go shopping. Their husbands sent flowers ahead to the hotel with the message, "Have fun. We miss you!" The Holy Spirit, living in us, helps us to love generously, and this brings happiness to those who love and are loved.

Joy. Ken was dying of cancer, but when I visited him shortly before the end, he greeted me with a joyous smile and a firm handshake. As we prayed together, his eyes reflected the deep faith that had been his life's compass. His daughter told me that as she had read Scripture to him one morning during the previous week, he seemed to be gazing through her into the infinity of God's peace. "It's so beautiful," he murmured. "It's so beautiful." The Holy Spirit brings joy into every circumstance of life, erasing even the shadows of death with the bright light of eternal bliss.

Peace. The Spirit helps us to live peacefully, to be attentive to signs of God's presence, and to find God in quiet places. Robert wrote: "I think God likes to do things quietly, as if he's sharing a secret with us. God mixes event, timing, and personal need to create a miracle. A miracle can be that unexpected phone call from a relative who says something you really need to hear when your hope is slipping. It can be a prayer or a poem or an article passed on to you by a friend with a message that hits your current problem right between the eyes. It can be the hugs and kisses and smiles of a child given right after the evening news just as you think the world's gone completely mad." Through union with the Holy Spirit, we find peace.

Patience. Lynne's mother died of ovarian cancer, after five years of suffering. Then her Aunt Mellany had a severe stroke and was partially paralyzed. Lynne visited her aunt in the hospital and complained that life wasn't fair: "Yes, we are supposed to imitate Jesus' suffering, but my mother suffered for five years. Jesus only suffered for three hours." Aunt Mellany used her good hand to draw Lynne closer, and said slowly, "Honey, it wasn't for just three hours. Jesus is still suffering for us." The Holy Spirit gives patience to those who suffer, and their patience brings peace to others.

Kindness. Beverly and Lisa are nurses who have dedicated much of their time to serving the poor under difficult conditions. When asked how she could be kind to clients who might be hostile and demanding, Beverly replied, "I pause for a little prayer before dealing with difficult people. It helps me to enter into their world and to be more compassionate." God is gracious and kind, and the Holy Spirit guides us toward loving kindness.

Generosity. In the first half of the twentieth century, my Uncle Leonard was the only orthodontist between Saint Louis and Cape Girardeau, Missouri. Many of his patients were so poor they could not afford to pay cash, but he never refused treatment. He often accepted eggs, cheese, fruit, and garden vegetables instead of money, and he built a chicken coop in his back yard to store feathered payments. He believed that the Holy Spirit had been generous in granting him the talent and training for his profession, and he generously shared what he had been given.

Faithfulness. Vic and Florence were celebrating their fiftieth wedding anniversary. "God has been so good to us, watching over us." Vic said. And then, with a smile: "Most of the things I worried about never happened." In their many years of marriage, and in the ups and downs of life, Vic saw the faithful Providence of God. Because God is faithful, Vic and Florence were faithful to each other. The Holy Spirit, living in us, helps us to be faithful forever.

Gentleness. A manager in a large factory had a problem with a worker who started drinking and missing work. The manager would ordinarily have fired the worker outright, but he had recently made a retreat emphasizing our need to bring Christ to the world and to be open to the Holy Spirit. He decided to talk to the worker calmly and try to help him. It turned out that in a space of twelve months the worker's marriage had disintegrated, his brother had been killed in an automobile accident, and his mother had suffered a heart attack attending the brother's funeral. The worker was given counseling by a plant psychologist, began to improve rapidly, and was later promoted to a higher position in the company. The Holy Spirit breathes God's gentle mercy upon us, and teaches a gentleness that changes hearts and lives.

Self-control. Pat was a successful salesman who loved his family, but he had picked up bad habits of smoking heavily and drinking too much. Finally, he realized that he was hurting not only himself, but his wife, his children, and his coworkers. He decided to quit smoking and drinking, and he did. When asked how he managed to succeed where so many others have failed, he responded,

"Prayer. I know prayer got me to quit smoking and drinking." When our own resources are lacking, the Holy Spirit helps us to gain control over the disorder in our lives.

UNION WITH THE TRINITY

Creation began when the life, wisdom, and love of Father, Son, and Holy Spirit willed all things into being. We, who were made to know, love, and serve God, discover that true spirituality unites us with the Trinity. In the Lord's Prayer we speak to the Father of life. In the Beatitudes we experience the wisdom of Jesus and walk in his way. In our relationship with the Holy Spirit and in the fruits flourishing through that relationship, we grow in love. There is no better way to fix our spiritual altimeters than by a life of union with the God who made us to be happy forever.

REFLECTIONS

While we cannot understand the Trinity completely, we can grow in our awareness of what Scripture tells us about God's inner life. How would you explain the Trinity to a child? To an adult interested in Christianity? Do you frequently consider God as a friend? Have you taken practical steps toward strengthening your friendship with God? What do you think of the way this chapter applies elements of human friendship to friendship with God? Which seem helpful to you, and which do not? The chapter speaks of "prayer that never fails." Do you agree that there is such a thing? Why or why not? This chapter uses the Lord's Prayer to relate to God the Father, the Beatitudes to relate to Jesus, and the fruits of the Spirit to relate to the Holy Spirit. How can all three Persons of the Trinity be found in the Lord's Prayer, the Beatitudes, and in the fruits of the Spirit? Can you think of people you've known who exemplify the Lord's Prayer as well as each of the

Beatitudes and fruits of the Spirit? Mellany said to Lynne that Jesus didn't suffer for just three hours, then added, "Jesus is still suffering for us." Jesus is now glorified in heaven, so how can he still be suffering for us?

EPILOGUE
The Search Continues

Happiness is a decision. The way we respond to everyday situations determines if we will be happy or unhappy. Sometimes choosing happiness is difficult. At Christmastime our Catholic Home Study office was closed for vacation. Enrollments, mail, and e-mail piled high during those five days, and I knew we'd be very busy trying to catch up. As I entered the office on December 27, Cheryl said, "Guess what? The server is down." A quick phone call to our computer expert revealed that he was on his way to another breakdown one hundred miles south. Well, at least we could open mail and correct papers on our electronic scanner. Penny turned on the scanner. "Guess what?" she said. "It's not working." We called the scanner company and the maintenance person promised to ship a new one by air. Then Cheryl's phone started to malfunction. We used another phone to call headquarters, which promised to fax instructions to correct the problem. We watched the fax, expecting directions at any moment. The fax rang, then sputtered, and—I kid you not—put its little feet up in the air, and died. Cheryl and Penny laughed and said, "At least the pencils are still working, so we can correct tests by hand." I, however, was not in a laughing mood. Feeling more like the Grinch than Santa, I returned to my room to work on this book.

And the first thought that hit me was, "Time to practice what you preach. You have a choice about how you take this. You can decide to be unhappy, or you can decide to be happy." I tried the latter. It wasn't easy, but I did decide to laugh off the day's foibles. At 6:30 A.M. the next day our computer specialist arrived and fixed the server in about fifteen minutes. By 1:00 P.M. the scanner company had air-freighted a new scanner to our office. We gave the fax a decent burial and ordered another. All those breakdowns were frustrating, but it did me no good to get surly. Choosing to be unhappy about the problems would not solve them. And so it is with many annoyances in life. We can choose to be happy and take inconveniences with a smile, or we can choose to be unhappy and make life more unpleasant for others and for ourselves.

HAPPINESS IS A DECISION

If we want to be happy, then, we must keep in mind that happiness depends for the most part on our own choices, not on the circumstances of life. Writing this book has helped me to see that every day I am free to make choices that promote happiness on each of the four levels, and to avoid choices that bring unhappiness. I try to reflect often on these facts mentioned in the Introduction:

> *It is easy to be unhappy. It takes no courage, no effort. Real worth comes from striving to be happy, from rejecting self-pity and the "feeling-good-feeling-bad" attitudes that bring misery to ourselves and others. We are at our best as human beings when we realize that happiness is largely under our control. Happiness is a choice to be made, not a feeling to be awaited. Great souls understand that they have no right to wallow in woe, because this makes others miserable. An unhappy parent places a heavy*

burden on any child. An unhappy child darkens the days
of any parent. We have an obligation to ourselves and to
others to strive for happiness.

At times this involves something so simple as deciding to smile rather than frown. A smile can be the sign of happiness, but it can, research has shown, cause happiness in ourselves and others. A smile can raise our own mood upward, and when others see a smile they tend to adjust their own feelings to match. I'm always pleased when someone greets me with a smile. I need to remember that Jesus wants me to bring God's love and joy to others, and I won't do that with a frown.

At other times our decision to be happy might require a major effort on our part and assistance from others. To move away from unhappiness, we might need to overcome some kind of addiction, to work through feelings of inadequacy, to forgive injuries, or to seek God's forgiveness. To move toward happiness, we might decide to enjoy the simple pleasures of good food, to rejoice in our own accomplishments and those of others, to strengthen friendships, to worship God wholeheartedly.

In every circumstance, ordinary and extraordinary, as we search for happiness and make the decisions that lead to happiness, we are never alone. We are in the presence of God, who made us to know, love, and serve him in this world, and to be happy forever.

REFLECTIONS

After reading this manuscript, Cecelia observed that it helped her appreciate the happiness she already has in her life and often takes for granted. Has this book helped you to recognize and appreciate the happiness in your life? Do you agree that happiness is primarily the result of a decision rather than of circumstances?

Why or why not? As you conclude this book, reflect on the fact that God made you to be happy forever. Place yourself in God's presence and pray the Lord's Prayer, addressing the words to God as a Father who loves you more than you can imagine, praying in the company of Jesus who died for you, aware of the Holy Spirit dwelling in you. You are praying to the God who made you to be happy forever!

APPENDIX
Scriptural References to Happiness

❧

G od speaks to us through sacred Scripture. Since God is not limited by space or time, God addresses each word of Scripture to us in a way that meets our needs here and now. In the passages below, God teaches us how to find happiness at every level, offers encouragement, and strengthens us in faith, hope, and love. A good way to use these passages is to place ourselves in God's presence and invite the Holy Spirit to open our hearts to what God wants us to hear. After we listen to God, we can then respond in our own words, asking God to help us follow the divine plan for our happiness.

The passages below are arranged under the four levels of happiness. Within each level, they follow the order of the books of the Bible found in the *New Revised Standard Version Bible* (Catholic edition). In addition to the citations listed here, readers are encouraged to look up other passages referred to in this book, especially the Ten Commandments (Deuteronomy 5:1–21), the Lord's Prayer, (Matthew 6:9–13), the Beatitudes (Matthew 5:3–11), and Saint Paul's listing of the fruit of the Spirit (Galatians 5:22–23).

HAPPINESS ONE

Genesis 1:27, 29: So God created humankind in his image, / in the image of God he created them; male and female he created them.... / God said, "See, I have given you every plant yielding seed that is upon the face of all the earth, and every tree with seed in its fruit; you shall have them for food."

1 Kings 4:20: Judah and Israel were as numerous as the sand by the sea; they ate and drank and were happy.

Psalm 104:14–15: You cause the grass to grow for the cattle, / and plants for people to use, / to bring forth food from the earth, / and wine to gladden the human heart, / oil to make the face shine, / and bread to strengthen the human heart.

Ecclesiastes 10:17: Happy are you, O land, when your king is a nobleman, / and your princes feast at the proper time— / for strength, and not for drunkenness!

Sirach 31:27: Wine is very life to human beings if taken in moderation. / What is life to one who is without wine? / It has been created to make people happy.

Sirach 31:28: Wine drunk at the proper time and in moderation / is rejoicing of heart and gladness of soul.

Sirach 31:29: Wine drunk to excess leads to bitterness of spirit, / to quarrels and stumbling.

Sirach 37:29–30: Do not be greedy for every delicacy, and do not eat without restraint; / for overeating brings sickness, / and gluttony leads to nausea.

Matthew 22:1–2: Once more Jesus spoke to them in parables, saying: "The kingdom of heaven may be compared to a king who gave a wedding banquet for his son."

Luke 21:34: "Be on guard so that your hearts are not weighed down with dissipation and drunkenness and the worries of this life, and that day does not catch you unexpectedly."

John 2:7–10: Jesus said to them, "Fill the jars with water." And they filled them up to the brim. He said to them, "Now draw some out, and take it to the chief steward." So they took it. When the steward tasted the water that had become wine, and did not know where it came from (though the servants who had drawn the water knew), the steward called the bridegroom and said to him, "Everyone serves the good wine first, and then the inferior wine after the guests have become drunk. But you have kept the good wine until now."

John 21:8–13: But the other disciples came in the boat, dragging the net full of fish, for they were not far from the land, only about a hundred yards off.

When they had gone ashore, they saw a charcoal fire there, with fish on it, and bread. Jesus said to them, "Bring some of the fish that you have just caught." So Simon Peter went aboard and hauled the net ashore, full of large fish, a hundred fifty-three of them; and though there were so many, the net was not torn. Jesus said to them, "Come and have breakfast." Now none of the disciples dared to ask him, "Who are you?" because they knew it was the Lord. Jesus came and took the bread and gave it to them, and did the same with the fish.

Acts 2:46–47: Day by day, as they spent much time together in the temple, they broke bread at home and ate their food with glad and generous hearts, praising God and having the goodwill of all the people.

Romans 13:13: Let us live honorably as in the day, not in reveling and drunkenness, not in debauchery and licentiousness, not in quarreling and jealousy.

1 Corinthians 10:31: So, whether you eat or drink, or whatever you do, do everything for the glory of God.

Ephesians 5:31–32: "For this reason a man will leave his father and mother and be joined to his wife, and the two will become one flesh." This is a great mystery, and I am applying it to Christ and the church.

HAPPINESS TWO

Genesis 1:28: God blessed them, and God said to them, "Be fruitful and multiply, and fill the earth and subdue it; and have dominion over the fish of the sea and over the birds of the air and over every living thing that moves upon the earth."

Genesis 1:31: God saw everything that he had made, and indeed, it was very good.

Psalm 90:9: For all our days pass away under your wrath; / our years come to an end like a sigh. / The days of our life are seventy years, / or perhaps eighty, if we are strong; even then their span is only toil and trouble; / they are soon gone, and we fly away.

Psalm 90:17: Let the favor of the Lord our God be upon us, / and prosper for us the work of our hands— / O prosper the work of our hands!

Psalm 118:25: O LORD, we beseech you, give us success!

Ecclesiastes 2:11: Then I considered all that my hands had done and the toil I had spent in doing it, and again, all was vanity and a chasing after wind, and there was nothing to be gained under the sun.

Sirach 9:11: Do not envy the success of sinners, / for you do not know what their end will be like.

Sirach 10:5: Human success is in the hand of the Lord, / and it is he who confers honor upon the lawgiver.

Sirach 11:17: The Lord's gift remains with the devout, / and his favor brings lasting success.

1 Corinthians 9:24–27: Do you not know that in a race the runners all compete, but only one receives the prize? Run in such a way that you may win it. Athletes exercise self-control in all things; they do it to receive a perishable wreath, but we an imperishable one. So I do not run aimlessly, nor do I box as though beating the air; but I punish my body and enslave it, so that after proclaiming to others I myself should not be disqualified.

Galatians 6:4: All must test their own work; then that work, rather than their neighbor's work, will become a cause for pride.

2 Thessalonians 3:7, 10: For you yourselves know how you ought to imitate us; we were not idle when we were with you.... For even when we were with you, we gave you this command: Anyone unwilling to work should not eat.

HAPPINESS THREE

Ruth 1:16: But Ruth said, / "Do not press me to leave you / or to turn back from following you! / Where you go, I will go; / Where you lodge, I will lodge; / your people shall be my people, / and your God my God."

Psalm 41:1: Happy are those who consider the poor; / the LORD delivers them in the day of trouble.

Proverbs 14:21: Those who despise their neighbors are sinners, / but happy are those who are kind to the poor.

Sirach 6:8: For there are friends who are such when it suits them, but they will not stand by you in time of trouble.

Sirach 6:14: Faithful friends are a sturdy shelter: / whoever finds one has found a treasure.

Sirach 25:9: Happy is the one who finds a friend, / and the one who speaks to attentive listeners.

Sirach 26:1: Happy is the husband of a good wife; / the number of his days will be doubled.

Sirach 40:20: Wine and music gladden the heart, / but the love of friends is better than either.

Isaiah 56:1–2: Thus says the LORD: / Maintain justice, and do what is right.... / Happy is the mortal who does this, / the one who holds it fast.

Luke 23:34: Then Jesus said, "Father, forgive them; for they do not know what they are doing."

Acts 5:41: As they left the council, they rejoiced that they were considered worthy to suffer dishonor for the sake of the name.

Acts 20:35: In all this I have given you an example that by such work we must support the weak, remembering the words of the Lord Jesus, for he himself said, "It is more blessed to give than to receive."

1 John 4:11–12 Beloved, since God loved us so much, we also ought to love one another No one has ever seen God; if we love one another, God lives in us, and his love is perfected in us.

HAPPINESS FOUR

Psalm 4:6: What can bring us happiness? Let the light of your face shine on us, O Lord (Grail Translation).

Psalm 9:2: I will be glad and exult in you; / I will sing praise to your name, O Most High.

Psalm 16:11: You show me the path of life. / In your presence there is fullness of joy; / in your right hand are pleasures forevermore.

Psalm 19:1: The heavens are telling the glory of God; / and the firmament proclaims his handiwork.

Psalm 32:1: Happy are those whose transgression is forgiven, / whose sin is covered.

Psalm 56:8: You have kept count of my tossings; / put my tears in your bottle. / Are they not in your record?

Psalm 84:1, 5, 12: How lovely is your dwelling place, / O LORD of hosts! Happy are those whose strength is in you…. / O LORD of hosts, happy is everyone who trusts in you.

Psalm 96:11–13: Let the heavens be glad, and let the earth rejoice; / let the sea roar, and all that fills it; / let the field exult, and everything in it. / Then shall all the trees of the forest sing for joy / before the LORD; for he is coming, / for he is coming to judge the earth. / He will judge the world with righteousness, / and the peoples with his truth.

Psalm 144:15: Happy are the people to whom such blessings fall; / happy are the people whose God is the LORD.

Wisdom 3:1: But the souls of the righteous are in the hand of God, / and no torment will ever touch them.

Wisdom 4:15: Yet the peoples saw and did not understand, / or take such a thing to heart, / that God's grace and mercy are with his elect, / and that he watches over his holy ones.

Sirach 11:28: Call no one happy before his death; / by how he ends, a person becomes known.

Isaiah 56:2: Happy is the mortal who does this…who keeps the Sabbath.

Matthew 22:37–39: He said to him, "'You shall love the Lord your God with all your heart, and with all your soul, and with all your mind.' This is the greatest and first commandment. And a second is like it: 'You shall love your neighbor as yourself.'"

Matthew 26:39: And going a little farther, he threw himself on the ground and prayed, "My Father, if it is possible, let this cup pass from me; yet not what I want but what you want."

Luke 1:46–47: And Mary said, / "My soul magnifies the Lord, / and my spirit rejoices in God my Savior."

Luke 2:10–11: But the angel said to them, "Do not be afraid; for see— I am bringing you good news of great joy for all the people: to you is born this day in the city of David a Savior, who is the Messiah, the Lord."

Luke 11:9: So I say to you, Ask, and it will be given you; search, and you will find; knock, and the door will be opened for you.

Luke 22:19: Then he took a loaf of bread, and when he had given thanks, he broke it and gave it to them, saying, "This is my body, which is given for you. Do this in remembrance of me."

Luke 22:41–43: Then he withdrew from them about a stone's throw, knelt down, and prayed, "Father, if you are willing, remove this cup from me; yet, not my will but yours be done." Then an angel from heaven appeared to him and gave him strength.

Luke 23:46: Then Jesus, crying with a loud voice, said, "Father, into your hands I commend my spirit." Having said this, he breathed his last.

John 6:40: "This is indeed the will of my Father, that all who see the Son and believe in him may have eternal life; and I will raise them up on the last day."

John 6:56: "Those who eat my flesh and drink my blood abide in me, and I in them."

John 14:2–3: "In my Father's house there are many dwelling places. If it were not so, would I have told you that I go to prepare a place for you? And if I go and prepare a place for you, I will come again and will take you to myself, so that where I am, there you may be also."

John 15:11–12: I have said these things to you so that my joy may be in you, and that your joy may be complete. "This is my commandment, that you love one another as I have loved you."

John 16:22: So you have pain now; but I will see you again, and your hearts will rejoice, and no one will take your joy from you.

Acts 13:52: And the disciples were filled with joy and with the Holy Spirit.

Acts 15:11: "On the contrary, we believe that we will be saved through the grace of the Lord Jesus, just as they will."

Acts 17:28: For "In him we live and move and have our being."

Acts 20:7: On the first day of the week, when we met to break bread, Paul was holding a discussion with them; since he intended to leave the next day, he continued speaking until midnight.

Romans 8:18: I consider that the sufferings of this present time are not worth comparing with the glory about to be revealed to us.

Romans 8:38–39: For I am convinced that neither death, nor life, nor angels, nor rulers, nor things present, nor things to come, nor powers, nor height, nor depth, nor anything else in all creation, will be able to separate us from the love of God in Christ Jesus our Lord.

1 Corinthians 13:12: For now we see in a mirror, dimly, but then we will see face to face. Now I know only in part; then I will know fully, even as I have been fully known.

1 Corinthians 15:54–55: When this perishable body puts on imperishability, and this mortal body puts on immortality, then the saying that is written will be fulfilled: "Death has been swallowed up in victory. Where, O death, is your victory? Where, O death, is your sting?"

Galatians 2:19–20: For through the law I died to the law, so that I might live to God. I have been crucified with Christ; and it is no longer I who live, but it is Christ who lives in me.

Galatians 5:22–23: By contrast, the fruit of the Spirit is love, joy, peace, patience, kindness, generosity, faithfulness, gentleness, and self-control.

Colossians 1:24: I am now rejoicing in my sufferings for your sake, and in my flesh I am completing what is lacking in Christ's afflictions for the sake of his body, that is, the church.

1 Thessalonians 5:16–18: Rejoice always, pray without ceasing, give thanks in all circumstances; for this is the will of God in Christ Jesus for you.

Hebrews 2:14–15: Since, therefore, the children share flesh and blood, he himself [Jesus] likewise shared the same things, so that through death he might destroy the one who has the power of death, that is, the devil, and free those who all their lives were held in slavery by the fear of death.

1 John 3:2: Beloved, we are God's children now; what we will be has not yet been revealed. What we do know is this: when he is revealed, we will be like him, for we will see him as he is.

1 John 4:16: So we have known and believe the love that God has for us. God is love, and those who abide in love abide in God, and God abides in them.

1 John 4:21: The commandment we have from him is this: those who love God must love their brothers and sisters also.

Revelation 21:3–5: And I heard a loud voice from the throne saying, / "See, the home of God is among mortals. / He will dwell with them as their God; / they will be his peoples, / and God himself will be with them; / he will wipe every tear from their eyes. / Death will be no more; / mourning and crying and pain will be no more, / for the first things have passed away." / And the one who was seated on the throne said, "See, I am making all things new."

BIBLIOGRAPHY

Collins, Vincent. *Me, Myself, and You.* St. Meinrad, Ind.: Abbey Press, 1974.

Komp, Diane M., M.D. *Images of Grace.* Grand Rapids, Mich.: Zondervan Publishing House, 1996.

Lukefahr, Oscar. *A Catholic Guide to the Bible.* Liguori, Mo.: Liguori Publications, 1998.

_____. *"We Believe..." A Survey of the Catholic Faith.* Second Edition. Liguori, Mo.: Liguori Publications, 1995.

New Revised Standard Version of the Bible: Catholic Edition. Nashville, Tenn.: Catholic Bible Press. 1993.

Schroeder, Gerald L. *The Hidden Face of God.* New York: The Free Press. 2001.

Spitzer, Robert J., S.J. *Healing the Culture.* San Francisco: Ignatius Press. 2000.

Swenson, Richard A., M.D. *More Than Meets the Eye.* Colorado Springs, Colo.: Navpress. 2000.

Ward, J. Neville. *Five for Sorrow, Ten for Joy.* Revised Edition. Cambridge, Mass.: Cowley Publications, 1985.